Praise for *The Secret*

"*The Secret Language of Spirit* is simply spellbinding. From the moment I started reading the first page I could not put this extraordinarily well-written and very easy to understand book down. William Stillman has brought to light in his own words all the hard questions we ask ourselves about our purpose here, what to expect when we cross over, and how to incorporate and communicate with Spirit and so much more. Fabulous, awesome and very informative on every plane of existence, a great tool for all metaphysical practitioners and novices alike. A must read for everybody."

—Bonnie L. Albers, internationally acclaimed psychic medium, and radio talk show host

"*The Secret Language of Spirit* is a must-read book for novice and experienced spiritual practitioners. William Stillman has an extraordinary ability to clearly describe spirit communication by utilizing current-day analogies that simplify complex spiritual concepts."

—Rebecca Austill-Clausen, award-winning author of *Change Maker: How My Brother's Death Woke Up My Life*

"A fascinating, well-written read from renowned psychic medium and spiritual counselor, William Stillman. *The Secret Language of Spirit* delves into the world beyond what we consciously know and helps us become more familiar and comfortable with the inner workings of spirit. Stillman's stories, insight and portrayal of spirit communication helps us understand the important connection available to us if we're open to receive."

—Dr. Jo Anne White, international best-selling author, president/founder of Dr. Jo Anne White Consulting

"*The Secret Language of Spirit* offers tools for decoding the veiled messages that surround us and offer guidance and hope. William Stillman shares the fascinating language of intuition and invites others to speak and comprehend it as well. This book is a must read for those who wish to better understand psychic phenomena and the mysteries of communication and consciousness."

—Lisa Smartt, MA, author of *Words at the Threshold*

"It is now time to speak to and hear from Spirit. This wave of expanded consciousness is exactly what we need to break out of our enslavement to matter and create a truly peaceful, prosperous self and peaceful, prosperous world. With *The Secret Language of Spirit*, William Stillman is at the forefront of this wave giving us the very skills we have been missing. We can now make this happen."

—Patricia Baker, creator and host of Supernatural Girlz Radio

UNDERSTANDING
SPIRIT COMMUNICATION
IN OUR EVERYDAY LIVES

The Secret Language of Spirit

WILLIAM STILLMAN

New Page Books
A Division of The Career Press, Inc.
Wayne, NJ

THE SECRET LANGUAGE OF SPIRIT
Original cover design by Amy Rose Grigoriou
Hand photo by Neo Tribbian/shutterstock
Birds photo by Fahmida Islam/shutterstock
Background photo by carlos castilla/shutterstock
Printed in the U.S.A.

To order this title, please call toll-free 1-800-CAREER-1 (NJ and Canada: 201-848-0310) to order using VISA or MasterCard, or for further information on books from Career Press.

The Career Press, Inc.
12 Parish Drive
Wayne, NJ 07470
www.careerpress.com
www.newpagebooks.com

Library of Congress Cataloging-in-Publication Data
Names: Stillman, William, 1963- author.
Title: The secret language of spirit : understanding spirit com-munication in
    our everyday lives / by William Stillman.
Description: Wayne, NJ : New Page Books a division of The Career Press, Inc.,
    [2018] | Includes bibliographical references and index.
Identifiers: LCCN 2017035958 (print) | LCCN 2017039062 (ebook) | ISBN
    9781632658845 (ebook) | ISBN 9781632651228 (pbk.)
Subjects: LCSH: Spirituality.
Classification: LCC BL624 (ebook) | LCC BL624 .S733 2018 (print) | DDC
    204--dc23
LC record available at https://lccn.loc.gov/2017035958

For Justin—
who is passionate about making the world
a better place

Contents

Introduction

Many of us studied a foreign language in school; perhaps it was Spanish, German, or French. By speaking a new language, we may identify the differences between it and our native language, including nuances in translation that don't quite match up. For example, the Italian word *zitto*, or "be quiet," can be interpreted as the coarser "shut up" in English. The many meanings for the Hawaiian *aloha* include not only "hello" and "goodbye," but "compassion," "peace," and "affection."

The majority of us probably learned another language for the duration we were enrolled in a class and then allowed our use of it to lapse. As the saying goes, if you don't use it, you lose it. But the more you *do* use it, the more proficient you become. This is how those who are employed as teachers, linguists, and interpreters (including those who interpret sign language) make it look so facile; speaking the alternative language has become second nature.

I've come to the conclusion that I am, myself, a linguist of sorts. As a psychic medium, I don't have a normal life or a regular job. In fact, my job is also to effectively interpret a foreign language, one in which I've become reasonably fluent. It is the language of Spirit. It is one of symbols and sensations, icons and emotions. I translate these impressions into words for those not yet as fluent as I am.

By immersing myself in the culture of the language, I've acquired a cultural competency. Thus, my spirituality is not a mindset, it is a lifestyle. I am speaking, thinking, and breathing this competency, which, in turn, complements a lifestyle that honors the culture. It is akin to becoming a first-time father; a good parent dispenses with self-centeredness in favor of making his child the priority. In my case, the child is my higher self. The benefit has been a greater knowledge and a heightened awareness of the Spirit realm. This comfort level has granted me tenure, yielding me confidence to represent this realm as an interpreter with reasonable authority.

As with any translation, some of it may be open to interpretation or personal preference. Ascertaining the proper terms that align with my own language can cause minor discrepancies, and subtleties may get lost in translation. For example, I was once asked by a woman from China to connect with her deceased brother. I was repeatedly drawn to the word *murder*, but she didn't understand this. I finally asked her how he passed and she replied that he had been hit by a car. I don't know if her brother's tragedy was accidental or deliberate, but the variation in semantics was interesting. In essence, I was being shown that he died violently, not of his own volition, and not from natural causes. Once the woman and I could agree on the generality of the translation, the rest of the reading flowed smoothly.

The closest approximation I can fathom for expressing how I interact with the Spirit realm is to think of it as a celestial version of charades. If you recall playing charades, you'll remember that the object is to convey to others, without speaking, a hidden meaning known only to you. There are some standard charades cues, such as pressing together both palms and opening them simultaneously to represent "book," or cranking an imaginary camera for "movie." If the hidden meaning is three words, you hold up three fingers; you fold down one finger to show "two" to isolate the second word. If one word rhymes with another, you can tug an ear as a clue to indicate "sounds like." This analogy perfectly describes my daily routine, continuously engaged in a celestial version of charades for advanced players.

The language I translate is fascinating and intriguing to me personally. I have long held an interest in the unusual and the unexplained. This interest was indulged and encouraged as I was growing up, so it comes as no surprise to me that I have composed a book about it. Here, I wish to share what I have gleaned from my years of interacting with Spirit— the compassion, the wisdom, and the beauty of its mysterious ways. Our everyday lives are teeming with information embedded throughout in the cryptic manner of charades. It is, in essence, hidden in plain sight. Unfortunately, much of that information has the potential to be disregarded or overlooked for being a secret language. My hope is that this book will provide the tools for decoding spiritual hieroglyphics as well as to offer insight about why Spirit desires to maintain open channels of communication with us all.

CHAPTER 1

Understanding Heaven

In order to grasp the concept of celestial charades, one must first understand the culture from which the communication originates. I have been privileged to experience vivid glimpses of what I can only deduce to be the Heavenly realm. It is an infinite space that well exceeds the stereotype of cherubs languishing on clouds. Instead, the Heaven I have perceived is quite the busy place with unlimited possibilities to feed one's mind and educate one's soul. Thus, we do not lose our identity as we advance to a new way of being. In soul form, we retain the wisdom of earthly lessons learned as well as the best aspects of our personhood. This transition holds promise for becoming an improved version of our old self. In short, I believe wholeheartedly that our consciousness outlives our physical form. You don't need a body to exist. Rest assured: You will still be you.

It's fascinating to reflect on the traits that distinguish us from one another. Our fingerprints, birthmarks, genetics, and facial characteristics may be wholly unique. Modern science gives credence to our individuality as spiritual beings having a human experience. The discovery of DNA has expanded the universe of human distinction as if to underscore the intelligence of our design. The same may be said for the composition of our very soul. It may be likened to the invisible equivalent of musical DNA. We are each assigned a note, or vibration, on a musical scale. Each of us is entitled to the space we occupy on that scale. Though the composition is dynamic as we each evolve, it would be incomplete in our absence. Not only is our soul energy unique, it is also indestructible and inextinguishable.

Most interesting to understand is that the Universe is not static; it is dynamic and imperfect! The Universe is in a state of constant evolution because every emotion, every experience, and every way of being contributes to its edification, including your own soul's contributions. As you read this, the Universe is expanding to accommodate tomorrow's thoughts and actions. There exists a perpetual cycle of shifting energy; in and out, coming and going.

Ever notice that newborns and the elderly require extensive amounts of sleep? Both babies and elders are in transition mode: The former group is acclimating to this new world and the latter group is preparing to return to the Heavenly realm. This is not to suggest that the gap in between is vacant or absent of communicative connection.

When anyone on Earth mentions or reminisces about a lost loved one, the emotion of the thought gets transmitted directly to the soul energy of the dearly departed. Think of it like this: When you post an old photo on Facebook, and mention a friend who appears in the picture, there's the option to create a link that notifies him or her of your post. Once apprised of the link, the friend has the option to comment or react in order to acknowledge their awareness and strengthen the memory. When this scenario occurs spiritually, the loved one's soul energy also has the choice to "comment" if it is deemed timely and appropriate, although it may occur when least expected. How the comment gets communicated is the basis for this book.

In my work as a psychic medium, the most frequent question I am asked about a deceased loved one is, "Are they at peace?" My first reaction to those mourning is encouragement to rely upon their own faith for reassurance that this is so. Clients also tend to feel worried that the loved one harbors resentment or disdain. There may be anxious concern about dissatisfaction with the memorial service or the dispersal of personal property. I can state unequivocally that these matters are of absolutely no concern to Spirit. On the matter of property dispersal, a woman's deceased husband once communicated through me in no uncertain terms: "I don't give a f*ck what you do with my sh*t." I was greatly relieved when she laughed and cried and explained that such a sentiment was putting it mildly coming from him!

Do you recall the first time you returned to your childhood neighborhood as an adult and were struck by how small everything appeared? Our soul evolves similarly, in the way we all outgrew clothing as our body changed and matured. If our loved ones have transitioned successfully, they now possess 360-degree vision. They have shed old ways of thinking and see clearly the grand scheme of the bigger picture. From their vantage point, they have released human holds and are granted unfettered perspective. It is like the satisfaction of finally completing a picturesque jigsaw puzzle; any disconnected fragments now make total sense. Oftentimes, this knowledge is borne of a consciousness accrued over many life cycles.

I can't say that we *all* most definitely live successive lives. As much as we are blessed with free will in human form, I strongly suspect that reincarnation is a highly personalized decision. However, I can't believe that the infant surviving only several hours after its birth is allotted such a restricted opportunity to know our world. Nor do I believe that human souls "come back" as creatures less than human, such as a cat. It doesn't seem rational to me that someone who has gotten so far as being human would regress to an animal form. But, I could always be wrong.

Some people require more process time to become acclimated to living in human form. They are called "late bloomers." They may be free spirits that march to the beat of a different drummer, shunning social conventions and manifesting brilliance in myriad forms. These individuals are better accustomed to existing as other beings in other worlds or operating on a level more conducive to the Heavenly realm.

Young souls tend to behave in ways that are narcissistic and reckless. These are often people who are greedy and manipulative. Young souls tend to be repeat offenders, making identical mistakes via variations on a theme, such as being incarcerated for the same infractions. They haven't yet learned to divorce themselves from the temptations of ego and are essentially the adolescents of the Spirit world. I have seen that young souls in Heaven require especial patience from their teachers. They are given role-playing exercises in an effort to educate them about altruism and sacrifice. Anyone on the earth plane who openly proclaims to be an "old soul" is in fact a very young soul that has yet to understand humility.

Old souls are those who sign up for struggles and challenging existences. They are often found in abusive, stifling, and oppressive environments, and may have impoverished and short-term lives. But being in the world serves a purpose, as their early demise often contributes to raising awareness or remediating issues that affect many on a global scale. A very old soul may be the person with Down syndrome who has limited speech ability but smiles at everyone he greets, the gay teen whose suicide affects his community at large, or the ill baby born into squalor with poor access to resources. I once saw a news segment on television that featured the medical trials of a family's young daughter. She was born with significant physical health issues including pronounced facial deformities. My first thought was that she was an old soul and that before incarnating she struck a deal to take on a very difficult life, but only if she had parents that absolutely adored her (which they did). A very old soul understands the beauty of sacrifice for the beneficial ripple effect it causes.

So what is Heaven really like? I think there is a consistent structure and a fundamental order about which personal perception may grant a measure of flexibility. This stems from how we were raised, what we were taught to accept, and any adjustments we made as we matured. If you've long held the belief that you arrive at the pearly gates, or you stand before your maker awaiting your spiritual scores, you will likely experience it in some semblance. Likewise, if you believe in a vengeful, wrathful, and punitive Creator, you may find your beliefs challenged. If the credo of one's spiritual belief system is "live to love" and "harm none," then it stands to reason that there is room for countless variations in perception.

For example, one core principle—for those who believe—is that when we die, we go to Heaven. But *how* we get there may widely vary from person to person. It may be that a loved one in Spirit arrives to escort us there. Or it may be that we go it alone as we travel down the proverbial tunnel of light. Some of us may be old hat at the transition process, knowing exactly where to go, like a little minnow instinctively making its way downstream. Others may be uncertain or disoriented, requiring a more mindful transition. In this case, a loving spiritual presence may gently persuade the newly returning soul to come along by safely escorting them to the other side.

Another essential belief about Heaven is that we are instantly reunited with our loved ones, perhaps even our pets. This can also occur courtesy of our personal filter. On a number of occasions in my meditations, dreams, and psychic work, I have seen an intermediary environment. This is an in-between place bridging our world with the next, being on the outskirts of Heaven. Here, there is a great meadow sprinkled with wildflowers, vibrant with perpetual springtime. The climate is warm, sunny, and comfortable. One's senses are heightened beyond anything we have experienced on Earth. It is like breathing fully after being congested by a cold or seeing clearly after the fog lifts from a steamy bathroom mirror. On the occasion I fortuitously gained a glimpse of this place, I vividly recall feeling as one with a waterfall just by observing it with admiration. I was joyful for the exhilaration I experienced as my essence danced with the cascading water.

I have come to understand that other intuitive individuals are also aware of this environment. It is commonly called Summerland. Its function serves as a gentle way to gradually acclimate an incoming soul to the transition process in a relatable setting. We have spent our lifetimes in human form, so it seems only natural that, for some, there is a reverse process to reacquaint returning to soul energy. After all, who could resist such a scenic vista with a forest of evergreens just beyond the meadow and the fragrant scent of pine in the air? I have seen people's dogs come bounding across the field to greet them, sometimes followed by one or two loved ones. So ecstatic is the reunion, that it only makes sense to continue the journey across the meadow without hesitancy or regret.

Elsewhere, in hospice settings, I have seen deceased loved ones slowly make their presence known to an individual preparing to transition. An alternate reality may crystalize in a new normal as the individual speaks directly to their deceased loved ones in the days or hours prior to their passing. It is a loving and compassionate accommodation that serves to soothe and comfort the individual. They may speak of readying to "catch" the train or taxi, and may seem relaxed, contented, and peaceful. The visiting spirits appear in an instantly recognizable form, though they look much younger. Once the transition to Heaven is complete, and the incoming soul becomes reacquainted, it is no longer necessary for a soul to project itself as human in appearance. Thereafter, recognition is discerned by the uniqueness of one's vibrational frequency, as was previously described. No one's identity is at risk of loss; it is every bit as familiar as recalling someone's face.

It is also generally agreed that we each have the chance to reflect on our human existence upon our arrival in Heaven. This is called a life review. But *how* this occurs may be individualized, as documented by researchers of life between lives. Some people report undergoing their life review privately, or in the presence of one or more spiritual allies. Others tell of viewing selections from their life simultaneously, or separately, on "movie screens." Some may be able to pause, fast-forward, or rewind these scenes, whereas others can manipulate the imagery to watch multiple variations on a theme, such as experiencing a momentous event from another's point of view. No matter the means, the outcome is intended to be efficacious and edifying, not humiliating or punitive.

The return to our origins coincides with a reunion of soulmates. A soulmate appears in our life in human form to support our purpose and advancement. This is a pact of pre-destiny made prior to birth. We tend to think of soulmates in a purely romantic sense; our core chemistry may feel interconnected with that of a partner or spouse. We may spontaneously laugh at the same thing or know what the other is thinking before it is spoken. We may feel as though we have known one another much longer than is possible. That person may indeed be a soulmate, but the soulmate association can extend well beyond its traditionally romantic connotations. In fact, we can have more than one soulmate.

A soulmate could be your sibling, your next-door neighbor, or a parent. Closely bonded friendships have coined the phrase "brother from another mother," though both persons are biologically unrelated. Think about old married couples and even some siblings that have spent their entire lives together and die days or even hours apart, sometimes in separate locations. Consider that in 2016, actress Debbie Reynolds passed away within 24 hours after her daughter Carrie Fisher.

I strongly suspect that we can have a history of previous lifetimes with a soulmate. I recall a psychic consultation with a client who couldn't seem to release an old boyfriend, even though she was in another relationship. I saw that, in a previous life, she was the old boyfriend's mother and he was her eldest son. He enlisted in World War II and was killed shortly thereafter. Thus, her inability to get over him in real time is fueled by guilt and grief that has seeped over from the prior era. Curiously, she affirmed that her old boyfriend is a huge war buff and he has compared her to his mother.

Your soulmate could also be your worst enemy. It's all about the intent gleaned from one to another in the relationship. I was bullied throughout my school career, especially by one boy in particular. He made life miserable to the point that I became suicidal. For reasons that still remain a mystery to me, he tortured me on a daily basis for many years. Decades afterward, I had a significant dream in which I was in a classroom as an adult. My bully was there, too, except he wasn't much older than I remembered him. I observed that his mother was cold, harsh, and inattentive, and I realized he must have felt he had good reasons for tormenting me. I was able to finally make peace with the situation. So, although I have forgiven him, I have also reconciled the probability of a soulmate dynamic between us.

As a psychic medium, I am often asked if we reconnect with deceased pets on the other side. I can only respond by relaying what I have been shown in my meditations and through my private readings. When we lose a pet as children, our family may console us by saying, "He's in doggie Heaven now." Curiously, this aligns with my personal visions about dogs, cats, birds, horses, reptiles, and a wide variety of other beloved creatures. That is, at the moment of physical death, their energy transmutes into soul form—yes, they possess souls—and transitions to the Heavenly realm, same as us. But what I have also been shown is that there's not a lot of commingling in Heaven between human souls and animal souls. I think we can reunite if we wish in order to re-experience the emotion and affection associated with a pet/pet owner relationship. But I think as a general rule, "doggie Heaven" means just that: a separate domain for animal energy. Take heart, however, if you are an avid animal devotee. I have also been shown human souls serving as shepherds and gatekeepers of that animal domain.

The interesting thing about animals, I have learned, is that they do not think in terms of the finality between life and death. They think in terms of an ongoing cycle of evolution. In essence, they understand the "big picture" better than most people. They are grounded in a perpetual meditation for existing in silence, and are readily connected to the Source. On several occasions, dogs have "told" me they were dying well before their owners knew. This was communicated telepathically in a way I would understand: They showed me a gorgeous orange-and-coral-hued sky with a gradually setting sun. This visual informed me that they were aware their time in physical form was limited, and that they were preparing to transition in a slow fade-out.

Their comprehension of how the Universe operates grants them great insight. This is why a dog that is in pain and dying, or is about to be put down, will look up at us with those big brown eyes and wag its tail—he already knows where he's going and is more concerned with comforting us! Deciding to have a pet euthanized can be an agonizing decision. But, of all the dog and cat souls I've connected with, not one has ever been in disagreement with his owner's decision. I can only surmise that the same holds true for other living creatures, great and small.

It is no coincidence that the infrastructure of our academic and governmental institutions is inspired by templates originating in Heaven. There are tiers of authority, planes of evolution, and counsels of elders, or patient, highly evolved souls. In the grand scheme of the Universe, we are all on a learning curve toward enlightenment. Some of us are preparing to enter college, whereas others are held back to repeat the second grade. In fact, many times, I have visited what appears to be an expansive university campus; all the architecture is bathed in the hue of golden light. Here, I have glimpsed the goings-on as I pass by the buildings. The walls are translucent and at first I was unsure of what I was seeing: classroom groups of what looked like frog or fish eggs. It took me some time to figure out that the "eggs" were souls, represented in a way I would recognize.

Oftentimes, these soul clusters make up a "home team" of personalities familiar to us. Though the outward, physical identities of each alter with various incarnations, there is no mistaking one from the other given the musical note of our soul vibration. I have observed the learning opportunities in which these clusters partake, sometimes in their classrooms under the supervision of an elder guide or teacher. Earth is the grand soap opera, and in Heavenly classrooms there are chances to role-play human dramas. Different scenarios are experienced on the order of coulda, woulda, shoulda, and good, better, and best choices. During these role-play efforts, souls swap places, assuming opposite genders and personalities for purposes of perspective-taking exercises. Soul awareness of another is like wrapping someone else's blanket around you and instantly knowing everything about him or her.

Similarly, I once saw a realm of purple, transparent bubbles. Contained within each was a movie scene all its own. The dynamic of each scene could be manipulated by adding other bubbles, which attached like the "twin" soap bubbles we blew as kids. One scene showed a couple having a bitter spat, but their energy shifted with the addition of a baby bubble. Now, they were conscious of not waking the baby. Their newborn became a focal point that dissipated the argument and refocused their attention in a positive respect. There were endless additions and fascinating combinations to be formed.

Other learning opportunities may occur in a vast library of archives. I later learned that, among others, Edgar Cayce, the famed mystic seer, also told of this hall of records. It has shown itself to me as a massive, golden, circular structure comprised of book shelves that extends upward as far as the eye can see. It is here that one can, in essence, time travel simply by thinking of a particular era when making the appropriate selection. It is very much like the books and paintings that are depicted as "alive" in the Harry Potter movies. It is an historian's dream come true. Many outstanding questions are answered here, as well as the chance to comprehend how parallel time-lines could have altered the course of history. As in the life review, there is also the opportunity to either observe or participate by reliving the events to underscore one's understanding. It is much like an interactive video call with historic personalities from old YouTube newsreels, documentaries, movies, or home videos.

Heaven is the place of universal understanding and forgiveness. As I previously alluded, there are no negative emotions in the Heavenly realm. The exceptions are being recalled during a life review or being replicated for educational exercises. Of course, not everyone who dies was a nice person or model citizen. But when souls deliberately blend their energy with others, the braiding instantly grants insight. This facilitates healing for those souls who are energetically damaged for having selfishly served their egos in human form.

Those who remain blocked after death, refusing to release earthly bonds and return to the Heavenly realm, are called "ghosts." It is a lonely, self-absorbed "half" existence, not fully human but retaining human form and thoughts. This can occur after a sudden tragedy because the soul is temporarily disoriented. If they remain confused, eventually a loved one or even an angel will come to retrieve them, although the best-case scenario is for them to leave of their own accord. Some ghosts hold back for being rooted in negativity: hate, jealousy, fear, rage, revenge, and so on. Still others thrived on destruction, and rebuke the notion of a Higher Power.

At the core of the most overwhelming evil there glows the tiniest spark of potential for redemption. What happens when destructive energies acquiesce and enter the Heavenly realm? One might suppose they are received with dread or apprehension, given a wide berth. But it is quite the opposite. They are the recipients of tremendous empathy for having lived such a blackened existence. The destructive soul energy is surrounded and embraced by wiser, more advanced energies adept at interfacing with such resistance.

The damaged souls are initially in the mode of old energetic patterns, and attempt to cause harm as a defense mechanism. But every destructive output is instantly transformed into something constructive until the damaged souls relinquish. In my meditations, this was illustrated with an analogy showing the three good fairies rescuing the prince from Maleficent's castle in Disney's *Sleeping Beauty*. Every effort by Maleficent's goons to stop the prince is thwarted by the fairies' magic antidotes: crashing boulders become bubbles, arrows are transformed into harmless blossoms, and boiling oil is repelled by a rainbow arc.

In futility, the destructive energies sputter to a halt. They soon surrender, having exhausted all options to no avail. They are then counseled by other energies that have previously lived similar experiences. A cleansing process begins by which these Heavenly mentors gently help to reshape, rejuvenate, and reform the destructive energies. The rehabilitation is then complete.

In the Heavenly realm, nothing is in physical form as we would recognize it. All we are exists in varied forms of high-frequency energy. As a result, no one has a body. We are absent of vocal chords and communicate purely in thought. It is an existence of color, vibration, and iconography. Thus, when Spirit communicates with those in human form, it must lower its vibrational frequency to accommodate our denseness. Oftentimes, these communications correlate with our human physiology (our senses) and our psychology (our thoughts, feelings, and memories). It is via these means that we may be poised to receive communication from Spirit. As such, there are telltale signs for the purpose of your existence embedded in all you see, sense, and hear.

CHAPTER 2

Ethereal Alignments

Some years ago, I was researching my book *The Soul of Autism* and stumbled upon the concept of entrainment. To distill the entrainment concept, it is essentially the synchronized, rhythmic connection between our internal physiology with the human heart. Symbiosis with loved ones begins with entrainment of the heart and mind in unison. It is from this entrainment, one to another, that our intuition reveals itself most gloriously. It occurs in ways that we might label "coincidence." Examples may include thinking of someone and, in the next moment, receiving a phone call, e-mail, or text message from them; sensing that a loved one is in distress and, upon reaching out, those suspicions are confirmed; or spontaneously laughing or crying with a loved one with no apparent antecedent. In layperson's terminology, this is commonly called "mother's intuition." It is a knowingness absent the mechanics of knowingness; it just *is*.

Entrainment can also occur between ourselves and Spirit. It is most readily perceptible for those who have made a conscious effort to become more conscious. The proper response to our humanity is to acknowledge that we are united as one. It's challenging to wrap your head around this perspective when one is not spiritually solvent. The greatest blockage to entrainment with Spirit is absorbing egocentricity.

As a matter of survival, we are born egocentrics. Our challenge is to shift from selfish to selfless. This is an individualized process. Some are incapable of achieving this process within the scope of one lifetime (such as the young souls previously referenced). For example, we all know toxic people who perpetually portray themselves as victims at the epicenter of real or imagined drama. Most of us attempt a balance between gratifying personal needs and sacrifice.

Creative advancements are made when free thinkers meet free spirits. In other words, when we are at our best, fueled by inspiration and confidence, we are actively collaborating with Spirit. When we create, we honor our very existence. The high vibration of the frequency we emanate is joyous, and cuts directly through the ethers to resonate profoundly in the Heavenly realm. Because the spiritual partnership flows so easily, there is little need for overt communication from our departed loved ones. They are already "feeling" the sensation of our creative process, whether it be self-improvement, higher education, spiritual aspirations, problem-solving ingenuity, and so on. But when we are blocked due to depression or serving the whims of ego, our vibrations become dull and muted, and don't extend as far into Heaven. The absence of expressive vibrations becomes cause for concern to Spirit, and it is then that an influx of signs, signals, and coincidences may occur. If we are not attuned to recognizing these communications, however, they may go unnoticed.

Another blockage to entrainment with Spirit is desperation that is borne of overwhelming grief. It may be a crippling prospect if the sole motivation in desiring to connect with Spirit is to revive the emotional sensations enjoyed in a relationship with a deceased loved one. It is advisable to wait at least a year after a dearly departed loved one has passed before attempting contact. The reasoning is twofold: to grant your grief perspective and to give the individual's soul time to reacclimate to the other side.

There is a video series on YouTube called *Channeling Erik* in which Dr. Elisa Medhus interviews her deceased son Erik, through various psychic mediums, on a gamut of topics from extra-terrestrials to celebrities and historical figures to explaining how the afterlife operates. Erik's colorful personality and off-color language has garnered him thousands of followers. During one of my psychic events, a woman's 20-something son who had also taken his own life, as did Erik, came through loud and clear. The woman was validated and attended my next psychic event with her husband and, again, her son came through. Among the validations, he made reference to his toy fire engine, which the family still had. The mother then came to me for a private session. When her son came through once more, he said, "Mom, I'm not Erik! Stop pulling on me!" I asked his mother if she was watching *Channeling Erik* and she acknowledged that she was. Her son was clear in telling her that Erik's thing wasn't his thing, and that Erik enjoyed being a pseudo-celebrity and facilitator, but her son wasn't cut out for it. He wanted nothing more for his mother than to accept his passing and move forward with her life instead of ruminating on his death.

Preparing for spiritual entrainment requires a reclaiming of the ability to view the world with the awed wonderment of a child. Each day holds the promise of potential for something truly magical to transpire. I recall getting for ready for school early one winter morning. It was dim inside and dark outside. Upon reentering my bedroom, I encountered a large black dog sprawled out on my bed with its head perked up, eyes gazing directly at me! It looked like one of the neighbor's dogs, although how on earth it sneaked into our house undetected and made itself at home on my bed, I had no idea. In fact, I even said aloud, "How did you get in here?" It took me a moment more to realize that the "black dog" was my winter coat, carelessly thrown where I had left it, organically misshapen to resemble a large canine. But for a fleeting second or two, it was real—an encounter that indeed felt so unusual as to be mystical.

My "dog" was akin to a psychological Rorschach test—a three-dimensional inkblot open to subjective interpretation. There's a similar occurrence when I see a bear's profile and a bantam rooster in the swirls of my poured concrete basement walls. It is this whimsical perspective that enables one to see the faces and shapes in clouds or concede that the classic optical illusion shows both an old woman *and* a young maid. Remember the "hidden image stereogram" or "Magic Eye" picture craze of the mid-1990s? A 3-D object such as a shark or a dinosaur would seem to magically emerge from the print of an intricate design if you stared at it long enough. In all of these instances, perceptions of what is physically seen with the eye and what is *perceived* with the eye are true simultaneously. Adopting this mindset facilitates a new understanding for all we survey. The random ladybug then becomes a spiritual symbol instead of an errant mite, as you will read later on. Prayers are answered with the clear vision of new lenses. And the synchronicity of coincidences escalates. It is entirely a matter of personal interpretation.

To connect, it is essential to unplug from distractions to create a state of solitude. This is akin to amputation for those who cannot take a leisurely walk without using a cell phone. To unclutter is to simplify one's space in order to just be. Alone, but sensing a Higher Presence. It is an opportunity for reflection and assessment. It is a state of mindfulness that emphasizes selfless over selfish. It is expressing gratitude for the blessings bestowed upon us, as fundamental as food, clothing, and shelter. It is a time for reconciling the three most powerful words anyone can say of ourselves: "I was wrong." It is a humbling.

Some enter into a silent state of reflection through prayer or meditation. But solitary engagement in one's most passionate activity is also a form of meditation. Think on the times you've been cooking, gardening, jogging, painting, or performing music and have lost track of time. Hours pass by in what seems like mere minutes. In these periods, our bodily functions are also suspended with no need to eat or use the bathroom. Our body is on autopilot. When you are physically engaged but your mind wanders, your energy splinters in the manner that Spirit can be multiple places at once. There is a shift in orientation, away from the physical but emphasizing the cerebral. Answers to questions may come. Problems may be solved. We may also find ourselves the recipients of spiritual wisdom.

During meditation, it is also possible to feel disconnected from your body, floating above it or moving away from it. You are experiencing the splintering of consciousness of which I just spoke. There is no need to feel fear or anxiety for being unable to find your way back. Our ethereal self, or soul, is tethered to our body at the solar plexus by a silver cord that is only severed at the time of physical death. I experienced one such sensation in early July 2007:

I'm lying prone but am levitating and begin to feel that I'm being moved, like I'm traveling backwards from my head end. I'm impressed with the thought, "Will you allow for this?" and, in my thoughts, I respond, "Yes, if it is for my greater good." The sensation of moving begins again and increases in momentum before stopping; it feels rather vivid. I arise before a dark brick building and enter. There's a landing with an upstairs and a downstairs. As the downstairs doesn't appear occupied, I take the few steps to the upstairs and enter what looks like a humble little small-town library. Behind the check-out desk are two young women, one of whom looks somewhat familiar; they are both plain or average-looking. We chat for a moment. I'm feeling somewhat bewildered, and I confide that I don't even know where I am. They tell me I'm in Canada! And I am so surprised to have traveled such a great distance from Pennsylvania in what seemed like a very short amount of time.

When one deliberately engages in meditative states of solitude as a matter of daily routine, an awakening occurs. "Don't sweat the small stuff" becomes more than a greeting card mantra. We are granted a new perspective on the Universe and our place in it. We may uncover dormant gifts and talents. We may find ourselves impressed with ingenious inspiration. We feel "lighter," think clearer, and find ourselves better able to make informed decisions. It is then, in this awakening, that we begin to notice the ethereal alignments that happen each day. These are common ways in which Spirit validates our presence and purpose. It is similar to the sensation I experienced not long ago while driving. I returned home using a street I previously only ever drove to exit out. Now I was on the same street but approaching from the opposite direction. It was quite odd although the only thing that had been altered was my personal perspective.

Altered perspectives and, by extension, altered states of consciousness, are at a fever pitch in today's world. Regrettably, too many are going about it through artificial and inauthentic means. Everyone wants to feel good, better, or "high." So many people seek to elevate their consciousness in ways that are quick and easy but, also detrimental and damaging. In the United States, we are in the midst of a heroin epidemic but others desire a similar effect through alcohol, sex, food, and gambling. These experiences cause a chemical reaction in the brain's neurotransmitters that raises dopamine and serotonin levels. These neurotransmitters affect pleasurable sensations as well as mood and behavior. Antidepressant medication has the same effect but many choose to self-medicate. Ultimately, however, inauthentic modes of self-regulation are destructive, not constructive. Research has shown that meditation achieves the same results by also raising neurotransmitter levels, especially serotonin.

Self-directed meditation may be challenging for some unaccustomed to it. The undisciplined may become distracted, the mind may wander off-track, and interruptions may derail the process. In these cases, listening to a guided meditation may be useful. Guided meditations may be found in books or on CDs, or downloaded from the Internet. For a guided meditation, it is important to create a quiet time in order to focus, allowing you to give your attention over to the process completely. There are no rules as to the length or duration of meditation time. It is an individualized opportunity based on your needs and commitment. Some guided meditations are intended to refresh and last less than 10 minutes; others may last an hour or more. A guided meditation is narrated by someone with a soothing tone who will lead you on a journey. You will be instructed about how to relax in order to prepare for the journey. From there, simply listen and follow along. I have found the best guided mediations to be those that walk you through it to the point of being "in the zone," then let you proceed on your own sans narration.

To prepare for writing this chapter, I reviewed my daily journals, kept many years prior. The entries document the alignments I observed as I was emerging and evolving. As I was without a mentor, I kept a written record to mark my course and chart my progress. Here are some examples. See if you share commonality with any of these instances of entrainment.

December 26, 2002
On drive home, was thinking about what Sherry told me about the cat; looked up to see large business sign, "CAT."

December 27, 2002
Looked at a return address on a card, which was the town Appleton; then looked down at a newspaper and saw the word Appleton. Thinking about warming my cold hands by running them under hot water in the moment I drive past South Water Street.

January 12, 2003
Walking the dog, I thought of the printer's secretary, named Jennifer. In that moment, I turned and saw a neighbor's license plate that said "JENIFER." En route to post office, I think of client M. Rainey. As I'm pulling out, I'm behind a car with license plate "RAINEY."

I have always interpreted these alignments as affirmation that I am who I am supposed to be, doing what I'm supposed to be doing in the moment. If you are also cognizant of such experiences, recall who or what you were thinking about in each instance. Chances are you were in a meditative "zone." Perhaps you were reflecting on a loved one, or had an altruistic thought like doing something selfless for a neighbor. Pay attention and see if you don't become increasingly aware of these little guideposts on a regular basis.

Your brand of meditation may be prayer. I have found the expression of gratitude and thanksgiving on a daily basis to be my personal, primary mode of plugging in. It is a great comfort to confide and commiserate with a parental presence, knowing that authority wants us to succeed by fulfilling our potential. To pray is to acclimate to the meditative experience. Here's a surprising revelation: If you pray, you are also practicing telepathy. Telepathy is a purely mental conversation by which we express our thoughts, feelings, and emotions. Our expectation is that our silent communication will be heard, received, and acted upon. If we didn't believe that this were so, prayer would be purposeless. But we pray with intention, believing in its power. Telepathy is the main modality of Spirit-speak. (This will be addressed in the following chapter.)

We may be born into the physical world alone but none of us is left to fend for ourselves without access to spiritual support. This support may draw our attention to ethereal alignments or aid us to recognize their meaning. In my experience, it is of utmost importance to protect oneself with prayer or meditation prior to engaging with spiritual allies. Where there is light, there is darkness. Destructive energies may manipulate and exploit the naïve or uninitiated. They do this by masquerading as something they are not, portending friendship, or making false promises. They may portray themselves as a departed grandma or even an angel. But because they are inauthentic, their masquerade will also be imperfect. The "angel" may give harmful instruction or "Grandma's" eye color will be all wrong. The most powerful way to hold them at bay is to illuminate the truth about one's own misgivings and shortcomings.

To deflect and repel such destructive energies, always encapsulate yourself in a protective shield fashioned of glorious, golden light. Do this simply by visualizing it, from head to toe. Doing this in concert with prayer is a powerful combination. This protection will aid you in discerning the authentic while blocking the deceptive. It will also make the distinction between the authentic and your own imagination. Once you enact this process, the likelihood of one's imagination intruding is minimized. Trust may then be given over to whatever may come.

Our spiritual allies are goodwill ambassadors. One or more is assigned to each of us. They are generally not known to us in this lifetime as a parent, sibling, or friend but adore us every bit as much. They may be thought of as mentors, guardians, or guides. Think of it like being a foreign exchange student in a strange land accompanied by a personal concierge. These allies are commonly known as Spirit Guides.

Spirit Guides originate in the Heavenly realm where the temperature is mild except at the line of demarcation with the physical world. When an intersection occurs there may be a draft, causing gooseflesh to rise with Spirit's energetic motion. There is no expiration on the contract with your Spirit Guides. They are divine agents of sacred resources, at your disposal. It is their station to impress inspiration within us; to function as creative muses; to aid us in decision-making; and to distract our attention to the people, places, and things that will serve our greater good, if we opt to avail ourselves. Thus, we have just as many, if not more, spiritual allies as we do physical friends.

Some Spirit Guides are like an amplified conscience, sort of an ethereal Jiminy Cricket. Others have as their area of expertise certain knowledge that correlates with transitions, projects, or directions relevant to our lives. If you are considering a major purchase, such as a new home, you may have a Guide who is real-estate savvy. If you are wondering about employment, another Guide, with background in the prospective field, may be a resource. If you are a poor judge of character, a Guide may step forward to aid you in determining someone's true designs on you.

Fitness of mental-emotional, physical, and spiritual well-being exponentially enhances one's susceptibility to perceive and receive. That is, the freer you are of vices and inauthentic distractions, the more you become an optimal channel. Desire will work in one's favor; desperation will not. For example, it is not helpful to make your commitment conditional by declaring, "I'll never do xyz again" or "I'll do such-and-such if you do this one thing for me." This type of spiritual bargaining is not conducive to connecting. It is not authentically motivated.

The same applies to karmic principles. There is a misperception that karma, distilled, means "what goes around comes around." In other words, you'll get what's coming to you based on your good deeds or misbehavior. But karma is not punishment, it is a series of teachable moments. It grants a new perspective when things go wrong. All that seems to conspire against you may actually be delaying you from uncertainty or even tragedy.

The most probable mode to connect with one or more Spirit Guides is through meditation, which further underscores its importance. The invitation may not be extended on the first outing; the introduction will occur in Spirit's time, not ours. It requires devotion and discipline. It may be useful to sense the gender of a Spirit Guide, or christen the Guide with a name of your selection. You may suspect that your Guide is a creature and not human in form. These questions will be resolved with successive meditations.

Personally, I am aware of four of my own Spirit Guides. The first and foremost is Frank, whom I named very spontaneously. The name was validated within the week when I answered a knock on my front door. It was a young man who explained that he accidentally backed the truck he was driving into my mailbox post and split it. He wanted to purchase a new post and replace it on his own time. He handed me his contact information and I later decided to honor his honesty and accept his offer. Not only was his name Frank, but his last name was Ward—a word in the English language, the definition of which pertains to guardianship and the act of keeping guard. In essence, his name translated to

"Frank the Guardian." When young Frank kept his word and returned, he told me he wasn't supposed to have been there the day of the accident; he was filling in for a sick coworker, and it was his first time driving the new route! It is important to note that Frank Ward is not my Spirit Guide. It's what he *symbolized* that was the intended communication to me.

Nora, another Guide, is a quiet, feminine energy who holds space mostly behind the scenes. Assa'd is a playful little boy with brown skin and big brown eyes. He thinks of me as a father figure and calls me "Papa." As I am without children of my own, his affection always makes me weepy. Once I discerned its proper spelling, I later learned that his name is Arabic for "happier" and "luckier," in keeping with his personality. The remaining Guide is not human but a massive white, winged stallion named Quicksilver. If, in meditation, I visualize mounting Quicksilver, he will power through barriers into spiritual dimensions that I am unable to enter on my own. It was with Quicksilver's aid that I first bore witness to the realm of purple bubbles containing movie snippets.

Spirit Guides will communicate by playing upon thoughts and feelings, senses and emotions. Spirit Guides may also cause a conjuring of memories to serve as metaphors to present-day circumstances, such as recalling a damaging flood when thinking about a souring relationship. Ethereal alignments are often the breadcrumbs tossed to us by our Spirit Guides in the hopes that we will discover the proper path, or make the best choice, on our own. These embedded clues are made specific to each one of us so engaged. This kind of enigmatic "Spirit-speak" is further explained in the following chapter.

CHAPTER 3

Spirit-speak

Not all earthly communication is written or spoken. Remember, Spirit usually speaks without talking. Spirit-speak is the native tongue of the Heavenly realm. This Spirit-speak may be cryptic, iconic, or symbolic. Symbols are shorthand for expressing bigger concepts or multiple meanings, like Egyptian hieroglyphics or even sign language. I came to recognize this in my work with autistic individuals over a 30-year period. Many such individuals are not verbal due to differences in neurological wiring. Contrary to popular myth, this does not negate intellectual competence any more than the person compromised by stroke or cerebral palsy. An argument can be made that those autistic individuals without speech naturally experience the same states of solitude that holy persons aspire to achieve deliberately.

The marriage of soul with flesh is something like a printing press; on occasion, the registration is misaligned, resulting in colors that bleed beyond the black outlines. Such is the case for those who are born with non-traditional ways of being, such as physical or emotional differences, like autism. A body that is physically compromised can usually accommodate a higher-than-average degree of soul energy. Therefore, people who are considered "invisible" are often the keepers of wisdom gleaned through careful observation, though they may be unable to express it through conventional means.

Like Spirit-speak, autistic communication often goes unrecognized or misinterpreted. For example, one mute man was preoccupied with a blue toy truck that he carried with him. The general interpretation was that his attachment was a reflection of his childish intelligence. However, the symbolic meaning ran deeper. The man had been inordinately close to his deceased father. They went everywhere together—in his father's blue pickup! An autistic boy seemed fixated on replaying one line from a Christmas-carol recording much to everyone's dismay. But the solitary lyric he repeated mentioned angels singing. Hearing it brought him ecstatic jubilance. One can only speculate to what he was made privy in those moments of ethereal alignment.

One little autistic girl banged her head more than 100 times at school each day. She wet herself regularly and smeared her feces around the doorframe of her bedroom. As it happened, she was in a state of great anxiety. Sexual abuse was occurring in her home, and she was in survival mode. She made herself undesirable with odor and posted a warning at the entrance to her room as a deterrent. Finally, a woman with autism, who was also blind and deaf, had the disconcerting habit of pressing her bladder, causing urination. She then smelled the urine on her fingertips, inhaling deeply. Of course efforts were made to extinguish this conduct, but her actions were entirely relevant. She had recently been relocated from the institutional setting in which she had lived her whole life. Without family photographs or home movies to trigger memories, she conjured a scent reminiscent of familiar surroundings to soothe her homesickness.

These are all examples of symbolic communication expressed by highly intelligent beings engaged in celestial charades. One can easily see, though, how the communication in each instance was misinterpreted literally as "behavioral" instead of authentic representations of importance. Spirit also conveys symbolic associations in similar contexts by using visuals, aromas, and music that, below the surface, hold greater significance. This will be explored further on.

One of the most spectacular examples of Spirit-speak was related to me by an old neighbor. Her father was a major league baseball player who was buried with a significant baseball ring on his hand. Later, on her mother's birthday, the ring arrived in the mail, addressed to her in a script not unlike her father's longhand. The postmark was indistinct, and neither the post office nor the funeral home had an explanation. On other anniversaries, a red cardinal would appear at their home (my neighbor's dad played for the St. Louis Cardinals). Another occasion, a single gardenia bloomed on a dormant bush; my neighbor's mother loved gardenias but couldn't grow them successfully. We can only imagine the kind of spiritual orchestration, effort, and energy it must take to coordinate the manifestation and timing of these communications.

Spirit communication has kept current with, and adapted to, modern technology. In rare instances, Spirit has sent messages to surviving kin using cell phones, e-mail, and text messaging. For example, when pagers were in vogue, there were reports of people receiving the numbers 07734 which, when viewed upside down, spell "hello." Still others have answered their phone to receive a very brief spoken message from their dearly departed. In these cases, the number from which the message was generated either cannot be traced or emanates directly from the deceased's defunct device. This happened to a woman I personally knew who received a phone call from her departed son's cell phone, which was in the same room with her, resting atop his cremains on her bureau! Unfortunately, despite her pleas of "hello, hello," she heard only static.

Curiously, the gap between Spirit-speak and human communication is narrowing, predisposing us to accelerated understanding. Internet journalism is rampant with bad grammar and spelling errors that would have been cause for embarrassment if not termination in another era. Just recently, I noted examples in which "bazaar" was used for "bizarre," and "grizzly" was used for "grisly." The thing is, few people seem to notice or care. Our rapid-fire communication via modern technology excuses typos, overlooks syntax, and relies on abbreviations. Instead, the focus is on how quickly one can ascertain the communicative content. I've seen this in word puzzles in which certain vowels are absent but our eye tends to automatically fill in the missing letters to continue reading fluidly. The most adept contestants on *Wheel of Fortune* are expert at doing this, as that is the object of the game. Elsewhere, most all of us have acclimated to the brevity of text messaging code, such as quickly deciphering "U R FNY LOL!" to mean "You are funny (laughing out loud)!"

When I was young, my mother brought home from a country auction a late-1920s children's book, *Story of the Merry Little Grig.* Its narrative was comprised entirely of written words alternating with rebus images, such as a drawing of a human eye for "I." This type of puzzle book may have been a novelty in its day, but I suspect that in the not-too-distant future many of our written works will be communicated in this manner for speed, efficiency, and global comprehension. To wit, our culture as a whole is shifting increasingly toward our own version of hieroglyphics by the universal use of symbolic communication: emojis!

Social media has given rise to the everyday use of icons that are universally understandable. *Emoji* is a Japanese term that equates with Greek ideograms, graphic symbols that represent an idea or a concept. Commonly used emojis include emoticons, or small cartoon faces expressing emotions correlating with the human condition: happy, sad, mad, laughter, and so on. After all, what could be more widely recognizable than a smile?

Similarly, pictograms visually communicate information for universal comprehension. The posted silhouette of a human figure wearing a skirt aids us in distinguishing the ladies' room from the men's. A stick figure in a wheelchair is shorthand for "handicap accessible." The image of a cigarette encircled with a red slash across it means "no smoking." Replace "cigarette" with any other image and the communication remains the same: It is banned. People without speech and limited fine motor skills have been using similar codes for decades to communicate wants, needs, and preferences. This can be as simple as pointing to "yes" or "no" written on index cards, or as sophisticated as touching icons on the keypad of an assistive technology device.

Decoding otherworldly language is the premise for the films *Close Encounters of the Third Kind* and *Arrival*. The plot of both movies deals with human effort to translate and interpret extraterrestrial communication. These films make perfect analogies for viewing Spirit-speak through an alternative prism. What we perceive as unusual and mysterious is the norm for those beings that inhabit supernatural realms. Thus, the supernatural is natural, and the paranormal becomes normal once we bridge the gap of cultural semantics. It is fascinating to consider the unlimited possibilities that await us once we attain this degree of understanding and fluency.

The wonderful thing about being human is that we are as unique and individual as each individual is unique. Each of us is hardwired with spiritual gifts and talents; some may be apparent while others may be latent. When it comes to tapping that aspect of our personhood, Spirit-speak will also be personalized by drawing upon one's points of reference and purview of life experience. When one is the recipient of this active dialogue, clairvoyance is key.

Clairvoyance is French for "clear seeing." It is the experience of receiving the visual impressions of mental imagery. Some of us are better predisposed to clairvoyance than others by virtue of being right-brain, or visually, oriented as opposed to more linear-thinking left-brain leaning individuals. People who are left-brain can "see" mental imagery if we command "picture this," but it requires concentration and effort. Therefore, if we direct a left-brain person to imagine a white house with red shutters and a blue jay perched in the green shrub next to the front door, he or she can visually conjure the setting if given ample process time. Right-brain thinking individuals tend to be artistic and naturally rely on mental imagery to correlate with their thought processes. Folks who are right-brain-inclined are often open-minded thinkers, whereas left-brain people are more logic-based, sequential, and calculating in their cerebral orientation. This is not to suggest that left-brain-oriented individuals are excluded from experiencing clairvoyance, but it may require greater effort to attain fluency, much like imagining the red-shuttered house.

There is recent scientific research to validate these contentions. As reported in the June 2017 issue of *Journal of Research in Personality*, researchers at the University of Sydney, Australia, conducted a survey focused on showing whether or not people who have a greater degree of open-mindedness not only have a better visual awareness but are also prone to visionary experiences. One-hundred and twenty-three students were given a binocular rivalry test in which they were simultaneously exposed to conflicting imagery: For two minutes, one eye was shown a red image and the other eye was shown a green image. Most of those tested reported seeing the images switching back and forth, as the brain can usually only process one image at a time. However, students who were identified as being open-minded also saw the red and green images fuse together. This mixed perception is not only an indicator for being creative and innovative, it suggests a propensity for mystical experiences. "At those levels of openness, people may actually see reality differently," said the University's Niko Tiliopoulos. "For example, they may 'see' spirits or misinterpret interpersonal or other signals." Interestingly enough, it was also found that some forms of meditation could increase the tendency for mixed perception during the binocular rivalry test. This concept will have bearing for the chapter that discusses autism, dementia, and mental illness, and an inclination for mystic or clairvoyant visions.

In my work as a psychic medium, I enjoy clairvoyant ability, but, then, I was always of artistic leanings. Over time, a core lexicon of visual symbols has been made apparent to me via clairvoyant perception. Of course, these symbols are all within the purview of my life experience based on what I have seen, lived, or been exposed to; otherwise it would be a meaningless exercise in futility. Many are obvious; others required trial and error to decode. Ultimately, they all make sense as metaphors or analogies—Spirit-speak in shorthand, just as has been discussed.

Some of the mental visuals are health-related. For example, when I am shown swollen ankles, it is my symbol for diabetes, a condition in which one's legs and ankles may retain extra fluid. A gas kitchen stovetop with a back burner turned on and left unattended conveys to me dementia or Alzheimer's disease, denoting debilitating forgetfulness. A large, gray letter "C" from which tendrils grow equals cancer. A small pink ribbon logically interprets to mean breast cancer. Children without hair refers to cancer, leukemia, or children with health issues in general. Rocking a baby implies a pending pregnancy. The exposed length of someone's bare inner arm, usually male, is my symbol for any drug harder than marijuana, such as someone addicted to heroin.

Some clairvoyant symbols are indicative of personality traits and temperaments. When I am shown an outstretched arm with an upright palm, it tells me there is a geographic or emotional distance between two family members (sometimes both). A man in military uniform who salutes is not only an indicator of having served in the armed forces, it is also a sign of respect for the recipient. Howdy Doody's beaming freckle face, of 1950s TV fame, tells me that someone had a carefree and contented childhood, whereas two rams aggressively butting heads is reflective of a clashing conflict between family members. Frank Sinatra singing "My Way" is my symbol for a dominant or strong-willed personality. A truck in a ditch, its rear tires spinning in mud without gaining traction, represents someone feeling stuck and stagnant. Television sitcoms, like *Hogan's Heroes*, or classic newspaper comic strips, like "Li'l Abner," are reflections of someone's good humor.

Large, rough male hands tell me that someone was known for being handy and mechanically inclined or worked manual labor.

Specific visuals are of a spiritual nature. A bouquet of roses, for example, is often given to the recipient from a loved one in Spirit as an apology or congratulations. Likewise, a birthday cake with lit candles acknowledges a family birthday, anniversary, or other celebration. A basketball scoreboard that rapidly accrues points until it bursts in a shower of sparks shows that someone has learned important spiritual lessons. Similarly, seeing a loved one in Spirit wearing a cap and gown tells me they are progressing and advancing in the Heavenly realm. Three-foot-long black leeches on someone's physical body indicate a negative spiritual attachment. Conversely, an immense column of luminous golden light represents an angelic presence. An ethereal male or female standing directly behind someone is my symbol for a Spirit Guide. On rare occasion, the Guides appear as twins.

My clairvoyant lexicon will most likely not be your lexicon. Spirit can only work within your personal frame of reference. That is, the more you know about the world, the more you will be privy to a broader array of inputs. Thus, the lexicon is not finite; the vocabulary will expand as you become more fluently proficient. The better educated you are, the more observant you are, and the more knowledgeable you become, the more you increase the potential landscape of iconography.

For example, I was watching *Antiques Roadshow* one Sunday evening, a favorite program when I catch it. I highly recommend it for its diverse snapshots of historical custom and background connected to objects, keepsakes, and heirlooms. This particular episode featured a reference to the African-American soldiers who served in the Civil War's Colored Infantry. I was fascinated, as it was something I had previously known nothing about. Lo and behold, 48 hours later, I was in a private reading with an African-American woman whose great-grandfather came forward and identified himself as having been in the Colored Infantry. To my surprise, she validated this statement. It was a distinction I wouldn't have been able to make two days earlier, but it was now part of my working knowledge base. The timing was impeccable.

Once you understand your own rendition of Spirit-speak, it almost becomes a fluid form of dictation. It is, in fact, how this book came to be written. Like mastering any language, an acquired fluency is at your total discretion based on what you invest in it. You may also find that you receive visuals paired with scents, tastes, or auditory sensations like hearing music that is relevant. This pairing of sensations will be discussed in Chapter 5. If you find yourself frustrated in your endeavor, take a break of several days and return to it. There is no rush or urgency. If, on the other hand, it comes hard and fast, you can always request respite through prayer and meditation if you feel overwhelmed. Your request will be graciously accommodated.

CHAPTER 4

The Significance of Three

Director Alfred Hitchcock, the cinematic master of suspense, once said that in order for an audience to retain a crucial piece of information, it has to be conveyed three times before it sticks. Perhaps this is the underlying purpose for the manifestation of Spirit communication in threes. Once or twice can be chalked up to coincidence, but more than twice is likely to strike us as unusual. The significance of threes is embedded throughout our culture and our lives.

Suffice it to say, anything truly mystical happens in threes. In fairy tales, magic wishes, charms, and spells traditionally occur in threes. (Most everyone recalls that Dorothy must tap her heels together three times to return to Kansas.) In mythology, the riddle of the Sphinx was a three-part question: "What goes on four legs in the morning, two in the afternoon, and three in the evening?" (The answer is man, crawling in infancy, walking erect in adulthood, and using a cane when elderly.) The proverb of the three wise monkeys is also trifold: "Hear no evil, speak no evil, see no evil."

A fundamental tenet of journalism is that written narratives have a beginning, middle, and end. This also translates to dramatizations presented in three acts. A series of three related, but separate, stories is a trilogy. In the creative arts, a triptych comprises paintings, carvings, or photographs arranged in a sequence of three.

References to three abound in biblical scriptures. The three gifts of grace are faith, hope, and love. As three denotes divine perfection, the number symbolizes the Holy Trinity for Christians. The ancient triad symbol represents the union of mind, body, and spirit. Thus, three signifies spiritual completeness.

Patterns of three emerge with irregular frequency throughout each day. The presence of three is so commonplace that it may go unnoticed and unobserved. In our physical world, matter is defined by three: vegetable, animal and mineral. It is said that all other numbers are borne of the first three. Triangles or triads (three joined symbols) have mysteriously manifested in crop circles, which are intricate designs appearing in fields, seemingly by unseen means.

Here are a few of my journal entries that note occurrences of three:

January 23, 2003

At about 4:45 p.m., I put the dog outside and saw three pretty bluebirds in our backyard. I remarked out loud to the dog how beautiful they were. I thought it unusual because I associate them with spring and summer, not the extreme Artic cold we'd been experiencing!

October 18, 2004

Taking the dog outside at 4:30 a.m., I thank God for the beauty of the new day and a moment later am rewarded with a shooting star, as per usual! Coming inside, I see the clock is at threes, also a very common occurrence, as it reads 4:44 a.m.

December 19, 2004

Outside with the dog and see three black crows fly by in a row.

January 24, 2006

Driving to the post office, I saw a single black crow. I thought, "Well, I can't *always* see three black crows together," and within a few seconds a bit further up the road, I saw three black crows flying together as a spiritual discussion on the radio said, "O Lord."

March 17, 2008
On three different occasions today, in three different locations, I noticed a single red cardinal singing as he perched in the top of a tree (the last place was the old willow by the stream—my favorite). Looking up its symbolism online, it seems to have spiritual implications.

One of the most powerful personal testimonies underscoring the significance of three came in November 2002. It was the week before Thanksgiving and for three days in a row, I saw a single ladybug. It wasn't the same ladybug and the sightings were in different environments each time. One appeared on the door of my father's house upon my arrival after a 90-minute drive. Then it stopped. As I was attuned to such things, on a whim I Googled "ladybug," "spirituality," and "symbolism." To my surprise, the ladybug did have spiritual significance in Native-American beliefs. Because its lifespan is so brief, the ladybug symbolizes releasing of frustration and trusting in the Great Spirit. This made sense to me, especially as I was two years into self-employment.

The following week, however, the communication of the ladybug had farther-reaching effects. I was scheduled to facilitate two days of autism consultations in a remote, rural corner of Pennsylvania. Each day, I would meet with family members mid-morning and then another group of family members in the late afternoon. On the morning of the first day, I received word that the family scheduled for the following morning would be unable to meet. I asked my local point person to request the family slated for the following evening to take the vacant morning slot instead. If they couldn't take the earlier time, another option was to postpone the meeting another two months. I would not be returning to the area until January. My plan was to then head home immediately after the second day's morning meeting.

As so often happens when the divine intercedes, things did not go as planned. The available second-day family was unable to reschedule to the morning slot. However, they did not wish to postpone the meeting another two months; they still wanted to keep their appointment for the evening of the second day. This disconcerted me, as it meant I would be idle for the better part of the second day. Though

I would rather have driven home, I acquiesced and consented to honor the meeting regardless.

I passed the time during the second day with some frets and regrets. Night fell, and I was picked up for the trip to the family's homestead—a small farm in a very isolated, rural setting positioned at the end of a long dirt driveway. The journey there seemed endless, complicated by a sudden snow shower. All the while I was thinking of home. We finally arrived and stepped inside. The modest home was warm and welcoming, with a respectable blaze glowing in the fireplace. The meeting concerned a quiet 3-year-old girl, who was also present.

Once everyone took their places, I was seated on a piano bench before the group. I took out my yellow ledger and began to gather information by making inquiries about the girl's abilities and passions. As I was taking notes, a small oval dot alighted on a corner of my tablet. It was a ladybug. I had not seen one since the previous week, so I was intrigued. Thinking myself quite clever, I silently thought the manifestation of two more would surely be a validating sign from Spirit. In that moment, a most peculiar thing occurred. Two dozen more ladybugs manifested!

A tiny army of beetles began to shower down upon me. I brushed them off my shoulders and away from the back of my neck. This was happening only to me, mind you. My ridiculous pantomime became obvious to the rest of the group. The mother was mortified, as it was my first time as a guest in her home. She offered a hasty apology, not wanting me to believe their house was typically infested with insects. By that point, I had a ladybug poised on my uplifted finger as I provided her with assurances. Having researched its symbolism less than a week prior, I was in a position to explain. "Because her life is so short," I said, "the ladybug represents releasing frustration and anxiety in favor of trust."

Not only did the rest of the meeting run smoothly, the importance of the ladybug's significance was revealed to me before I departed. This was a family in turmoil. In particular, the marriage had been struggling. The mother told me that she had been planning to file for divorce after the holidays. The reason she had taken no action beforehand was because her family was waiting on this meeting with me— the meeting I didn't want to go to and attempted to postpone another two months. The family was prepared to persevere now that some simple truths were illuminated about disposing of unfounded fears and uniting through trust and resolve. The symbolism of the ladybug wasn't for me, necessarily, it was intended for this family. I was merely the interpreter.

b.

in ma..

shared this ..

bugs will appear a..

of perpetuating its me..

out of an auditorium, having just finished retelling the account, and others directed my attention to a large chandelier just outside the doorway. Believe it or not, it was covered with dozens of ladybugs, and this was in the middle of winter.

Threes often appear numerically. With the advent of digital clocks, it is possible to casually glance up, or wake up, to see a triple-digit time comprised of the same number. These are 1:11, 2:22, 3:33, 4:44, and 5:55. Thus, there are 10 instances lasting 60 seconds each throughout a 24-hour period in which to see these alignments. It doesn't matter that the time is precisely 2:22 as it pops up on a clock, when elsewhere it registers accurately as 2:21 or 2:23. What matters is what you personally perceive in the moment of synchronicity.

Reflect on those occasions when you looked at the time, received a text message, or got an e-mail stamped with one of those mysterious three-digit numerals. Did viewing the time in those moments by chance correspond with hearing from a loved one or thinking optimistic thoughts? In fact, as I write this, an e-mail came in at 2:22 p.m. with a loving message from a new acquaintance. I found other examples of this occurring when I reviewed my old journal logs.

On May 12th, 2004, I recorded this entry: "I awakened at 3:33 a.m., got up and when I came back to bed the clock read 4:44 a.m." Curiously, this was precisely three months prior to the start of my professional career as a psychic. In early 2008, I had a spate of awakening to the times 2:22 or 4:44 a.m. Then on March 24th, I awakened at 2:22 a.m. having just had a dream in which I was instructing or counseling a group of adults. The following October 27th, I spoke at a conference about spiritual giftedness for the first time in a mainstream forum. Although I was wary of the response, the evaluation feedback was praiseworthy and I arrived home at exactly 3:33 p.m.

As I conduct psychic readings, I keep a small clock in front of me on the table so as to keep track as each session progresses. Oftentimes, I will finish delivering an empowering message or channeling an emotional communication from Spirit only to notice that the time is 2:22 or 3:33 and so on. I always bring this to a client's attention. It serves to accentuate or punctuate the moment so beautifully. As you become increasingly aware, the prevalence of the

~s may well serve to validate you as
me.

~hree-digit numbers are of the
~ntion to the appearance of
~rhaps represent a deceased
loved one's lucky numbers, consistently played lottery numbers, or birth day and month. For example,
someone's April 23rd birthday would show digitally
as 4:23. The number 939 is the closest clock approximation to 1939, a year that holds special importance
to me. I tend to see 939 when I am thinking thoughts
coinciding with 1939.

A close friend and I have a secret code that is the
number 317. It is taken from a line in a play with
which we both connect happy memories. As some
people reminisce. "They're playing our song," so
have we designated 317 as "our" number. It appears to
follow us uniquely. It is surprising how often 317 turns
up randomly (or seemingly so) to reinforce the bond
in our relationship. One of us usually brings it to the
other's attention in the moment it transpires, especially when we are parted. It shows on digital clocks
as 3:17 or turns up on license plates or hotel rooms.

What are the odds that exact number, and all it
represents, would make its presence known to us so
frequently? We don't seek it out; it finds us organically. It is a pleasing, comforting thing that validates

our union. At least that is how we choose to interpret those instances of synchronicity. I suspect that when one of us passes away, 317 will serve as a spiritual calling card—a powerful command of symbolism that distills an emotional connection to those three numerals. Curiously, the birthday of the actress who originated the role in which she sings "317" is 2/22 or February 22nd.

The number 666 is also a three-digit numeral but that which traditionally holds fearful connotations. The essence of human wisdom also entails imperfection. Thus, 666 is a manmade number. It is a number to which we have ascribed negative human emotions: dread, anxiety, fright, and so on. We have wrongly given 666 power by channeling negative thoughts and feelings into its representation. It will become what that energy creates, fosters, and sustains. Disempower 666 by relinquishing any power it may have over you. It is a superstition every bit as much as people fear and avoid the number 13.

The ability of Spirit to communicate using the symbolism of three extends beyond the will of human souls to include those of our animal companions as well. One extraordinary example of this manifestation occurred for Jofa following the passing of "Sweetie," her beloved West Highland White Terrier. Sweetie was 14 when she passed the day before Thanksgiving 2013, but it wasn't until three years later that Jofa "heard" from Sweetie in a tangible way. While cleaning behind her dining room curtain, Jofa found a Milk-Bone dog biscuit, though she had cleaned there many times since Sweetie's passing. Stranger still is that Sweetie disliked Milk-Bones and refused to eat them, so they were not kept in the house. Two weeks later, Jofa discovered a second Milk-Bone, this time in her closet behind a box that she had previously moved. Less than a month later, Jofa's daughter was visiting with her dog, Bernie, who sleeps in Sweetie's old bed. Bernie began spontaneously digging at something in the bed that turned out to be a third Milk-Bone! No more Milk-Bones have appeared since then, and all three Milk-Bones were different colors, the last one being red—which is fitting as Milk-Bone incorporates two hearts into the design stamped on the surface of each biscuit.

Where the significance of three is concerned, "There are three aspects to everything and anything," writes P.M.H. Atwater, LHD, one of the original researchers in the field of near-death studies and the author of 15 books, including *A Manual for Developing Humans*. "We can look at and deal with things on the conscious level, or the subconscious level, or the superconscious level." Atwater continues, "Each aspect denotes a step up in our consciousness, our experience of the world, and in our awareness of who we really are. For instances, someone communicating at third-level reality will not be understood by someone at first level. If we could just understand that alone, we could better understand our differences and how we live."

Part of my own lifestyle is to devote intervals throughout each day to introspection. As previously stated, this includes prayer and meditation. When I am providing a service to others, be it a private consultation or speaking with an audience, I also recite a blessing to ensure purity and protection in the interaction. The blessing includes language of equal portions that covers our concept of time's three domains: past, present, and future. The recitation is intended to encompass the mystical for all that we have been, all that we are presently, and all that we are becoming.

It is a hallmark of spiritual maturity to forgive and forget, and to not dwell in the past. It would be a detriment to ruminate on your 20s if you are twice that age or more. But when we think on all that we have been, as in the initial aspect of my blessing, it grants us the perspective of progress. We should be continuously advancing forward in an affirmation of our respective being-ness. Otherwise, we'd be in a mental-emotional, physical, and spiritual state of arrested development, stagnant and afraid. If you have made great strides to improve yourself, acknowledge your achievements and grant credit to yourself for having overcome obstacles.

Reflecting on who we are presently is the second aspect of the blessing. It is an opportunity to express praise, gratitude, and thanksgiving. It is atonement for being present in the moment. Assess the gifts and blessings and privileges you enjoy right now, even if it is as seemingly simple as being able to breathe fresh air independently. Focus not on the past or future, but on the moment of spiritual connectivity. Perhaps you are feeling the presence of a Spirit Guide or another authentic power. Allow this sensation of harmony to disperse and radiate from your core until it holds good and great influence over others with whom you are associated.

If you embrace these ideologies, then you are in the act of becoming, which is the third portion of the blessing. You are not fixated on the past. And although you appreciate the present, you are also aware of being a work in progress. This involves due regard for growing, learning, and expanding your purview of awareness. This is spiritual evolution. This is becoming.

Use this concept when setting intentions of personal deliberation. The first portion (all that you have been) initiates the idea; the second (all that you are presently) affirms the intention; and the third (all that you are becoming) projects its future fulfillment. If this is a loyal commitment, and not a quick fix or a temporary fad, it will bear fruit. If you are seeking a tangible validation, patiently wait until you see threes. This may come as three like animals or three birds or insects, such as three butterflies. Or you might see a succession of threes, such as seeing or hearing the same word, number, or phrase repeatedly. When this occurs, pause to ascertain the authenticity of the validation using your own intuition. Permit time for it to resonate within. If it makes sense, use and retain it for future reference. If not, simply discard it and await another sign in Spirit-speak jargon.

CHAPTER 5

Aromatic Sensitivity and Musical Attunement

Spirit's efforts to comfort and communicate can often play upon our personal physiology. The very cells of our physical body record and retain information gleaned from our individual life journey—good, bad, and indifferent. We are a walking testimony to our own history of being in the world. It makes sense, then, that our ethereal allies would work with our mental-emotional, physical, and spiritual composition. This occurs gently, subtly, and respectfully so as not to cause alarm or disruption. Remember, a loving presence will only ever be a loving presence. Therefore, a loving presence operates in ways befitting a kinship bonded in all that is right and true and good and kind. A loving presence works subliminally, in the background, so as to remain unobtrusive but with enough visibility to create an impression, as you will read.

Our senses often trigger memories and emotions connected to memories. How many of us have inhaled the scent of perfume, after-shave, tobacco, or a cooking odor and immediately thought of a deceased loved one? It is a unique and personal experience. Because it is meaningful, it initiates emotional memories. The emotional memories correspond to the scents. Olfactory retention is the strongest of identifying senses correlated to memory. A specific smell can trigger trauma, cause a chortle, or bring us to tears. In psychic terminology, the inexplicable sensation of aromas without a legitimate source is called clairalience.

Oftentimes before an event, I begin to sense the presence of Spirit hours in advance. Sometimes it is while I am in the bathroom preparing for the day or while taking a shower. Other times I may feel impressed with information on a meditative walk. On occasion, I have felt something, or someone, in the passenger seat of my car en route to the venue. Such was the case one January afternoon. What follows is an instance in which I served as the intercessor. A certain scent manifested memories that were not my own. The intent was for me to convey its relevance to a third party.

As I was traveling through Pennsylvania farm country, I caught a fleeting whiff of cow manure—very common for the region. But then I began to feel a mother memory connected to the manure smell. I was shown that, as a girl, the mother was expected to help out by milking cows that were sometimes uncooperative. I was next shown one belligerent bovine kicking over a bucket of precious milk and was told, "Where do you think the saying 'kick the bucket' comes from?" I was also getting a "D" name, like Dolly, associated with this. As if to reinforce the moment, my car's vent fan, that had been directed at my cold feet, suddenly switched settings and now blew the manure scent in my face. Once the event actually commenced, I told the audience of my experience. Sure enough, only one woman connected with the information. There had indeed been a Dolly in the family who was now deceased. Not only that, she was, herself, a "D" name. She affirmed that her mother had milked cows as a girl and was affectionately called "Manure Mom" for an old snapshot of her posed next to a bag of cow dung!

Cooking odors are commonplace. Some of our best and most pleasant memories are associated with family gatherings at birthdays, anniversaries, and holidays over which we break bread. Some of our dearly departed had reputations for preparing food with such style and passion that certain dishes were second to none for the expertise of their culinary excellence. When I am engaged with conveying celestial charades, I often smell bread, pasta with homemade sauce, cakes, and cookies made from scratch. The recipient of this information usually verifies the connection between the food aroma and the person who has passed on. The happiest part of this experience is that many times, the mother, grandmother, or great aunt will "make" something special to honor me, too! Incidentally, the simulation of "taste" on one's tongue is called clairgustance. For me, it doesn't occur as often as receiving aromas and it's not always as pleasant, such as the times I've tasted blood, which indicates the injuries of someone who passed in a collision or, sadly, someone who took his own life by inserting a gun barrel in his mouth and pulling the trigger.

On numerous occasions, I have also had it happen that these mother-figures-in-Spirit draw my attention to their old, time-honored recipes. Usually, these recipes have been handed down in the family and are in the possession of, or easily accessed by, a client. The way it's been explained to me, the emphasis is not on recognizing the recipe(s) as much as it's about appreciating the emotional connection in memory. The experience of enjoying good food in good company is key. It is not just a gathering, it is a communion. The spiritual significance occurs when the family recipe is reenacted. When this happens, it organically conjures those associative memories and the emotion of such gets imbued into the very food itself. This, in turn, is consumed by all who take pleasure in eating the food. In this manner, the recipe *and* the loving emotion, associated in memory with it, is passed along. The spiritual simplicity of the concept is beautiful.

Just recently, I was in a private session with a woman who was born in Thailand. I am remiss in knowing little to nothing about Thai culture, customs, or cuisine. Nonetheless, this woman's very strong, dominant grandmother came barreling through me. I should note that she was not English-speaking; fortunately, however, my Spirit Guides know how to use Google Translate. She was full of praise and admiration for all of her granddaughter's accomplishments. As a reward to me for being the channel, the grandmother began making me her specialty: a spicy rice concoction wrapped in banana leaves. When I communicated this to my client, it was soundly validated! I had no idea and no prior point of reference for this; I could only describe what I was seeing and smelling. But, it served to prove Spirit's presence.

On another occasion, a motherly presence indicated that her form of Spirit-speak, to alert loved ones of her nearness, was the scent of her perfume. She was very specific, however, and kept showing me the word *white*, and a white flask of Kouros, a cologne that I personally wore decades prior. When I communicated this information, my client blurted out that his mother was fond of, and had used, White Diamonds perfume. Similarly, a client's deceased father once overwhelmed me with the smell of Old Spice aftershave. It was so distinctive as to be almost comical, as if he received it as a gift and felt obliged to douse himself with it so that there would be no mistaking its aroma. The client said that, as a girl, she did remember giving her father Old Spice for a Christmas present. It was not her father's favorite, but he was good-natured enough to use it then, and was playfully ribbing her about it now.

Not everything is something, however. Not every random whiff of Chanel No. 5 is Grandma, especially if you've just walked past the department store perfume counter. But if you smell Grandma's Chanel while gardening or making the bed, that's another matter. On those occasions when you have been so pleasantly surprised, consider where you were and what you were doing. It is likely that you were on auto-pilot, driving or engaged in some routine activity. Had the specific loved one with whom you associate a certain aroma been in your thoughts recently? Does it herald a birthday, anniversary, or celebration? Or have you been struggling to reconcile your emotions of late? Chances are the pleasing scent had soothing properties or, in the case of the manure, a strong association linked in memory.

A single song can unite us by expressing what many feel. Music is a universally understood language. Certain musical compositions can energize or evoke melancholia. It's actually quite extraordinary that an arrangement of musical notes can elicit a range of human emotional responses. But recall the analogy that each of us corresponds to a unique spiritual note on a grand scale. Given this understanding, it is then reasonable that music should strike a resonate chord. Indeed, in a recent meditation, I returned to Summerland and entered a buff-colored music auditorium from which emanated glorious vibrations. I tried to remain inconspicuous, wishing merely to observe without being intrusive, but I was instantly made to feel welcome. Beyond that, I was impressed with the sensation that my presence was not only expected but my inclusion was necessary to the emerging musical composition. It was a feeling of total acceptance, and I was honored to make my contribution to the whole.

Where the concept of celestial charades is concerned, music plays a significant role. Like emojis and emoticons, music is spiritual shorthand. That is, a byte of music can convey many meanings in a compressed format. For example, I once conducted a psychic event in which a mother came through in Spirit. It began with the strong smell of cigarettes paired with the word *daughter.* At first, I thought it meant someone had lost a daughter, but a woman raised her hand, and said *she* was the daughter and her mother had been the chain-smoker. Her mother directed my attention to a Barry Manilow song. But the daughter couldn't validate any connection. I was grasping until I was shown a sunrise. I asked, "Who's the Barry Manilow fan?" and another woman raised her hand. I asked about a Manilow song with the word *day* in it, and she immediately called out "Daybreak." That still made no sense to the daughter.

A quick-thinking friend Googled the lyrics on the spot. The song speaks of optimism and inviting Spirit in. It goes on to implore a time for believing instead of grieving. The chorus is jubilant about letting belief shine all around the world. The daughter revealed that her mother had died less than 24 hours prior. She was struggling emotionally as well as trying to juggle a family dispute with the logistics of planning a memorial service. The song encapsulated her circumstances with a plea for faith. The defining moment came when I next heard Frank Sinatra singing "My Way." The woman and her husband about fell out of their seats. It was the very song the mother had requested to be played at her funeral.

"Hearing" music or otherwise untraceable sounds is known as clairaudience. Be mindful that it may not be solely the song that is the intended communication from Spirit. The title alone, the lyrics, and even the name of the artist could hold relevance to an association in memory. For instance, picking up on country-western singer Brad Paisley could be interpreted as an indication for the name "Brad," or a reference to the paisley patterns preferred by a deceased loved one. Other times, the synchronicity of the song could serve as one of spiritual affirmation—another guidepost to reinforce your purpose for being in the moment. You may be thinking of your Spirit Guide and hear the Doobie Brothers singing about where you would be now without love. You would be accurate in accepting this as a validation. I experienced a small flurry of such seeming coincidences in 2003:

March 18, 2003
Driving to Doylestown, was thinking of the song "Bennie and the Jets," a few moments

later, I heard it on the radio. On the drive home, I heard Three Dog Night's "Old Fashioned Love Song." I thought about listening to an old 45-rpm record growing up in which there was a musical improvisation on it, but I never heard that version of the song on the radio. I sang it and a moment later that version played.

July 7, 2003

En route to the airport shuttle parking, I thought about 9/11 and, in particular, the song "Have You Forgotten?" by a country-western singer. I had only heard it once before but, within minutes, I boarded the shuttle and this song was playing on the radio (it's not a new song).

July 15, 2003

Driving back from the post office, I saw a girl walking alongside the road going to work at Taco Bell. I said, "God bless you" in my thoughts to her, and, a second later, the song on the radio said, "blessed her."

August 28, 2003

Driving home, I thought of Jessica and her baby, Isabella (whose name I couldn't recall recently). I then sang a bit of Bjork's song "Isobelle." Coming home, I had an e-mail from Jessica with baby pictures.

In these instances, you can see the lineage between emotional ties, memories, or compassionate connections, and the personalized instance of celestial charades in the moment. It is all very fitting, as if to underscore or validate the experience. You may have similar examples yourself, or you may be intrigued to learn more about it.

In keeping with the notion that Spirit works with our personal physiology, it may be useful to know who among us is optimally predisposed. Usually, this predisposition includes sensitivity across four domains: two physical domains, one mental-emotional domain, and one spiritual domain.

- Emotional Sensitivity: prone to become emotionally moved, overcome, or overwhelmed in response to viewing material, interactions in relationships, music, and/or spiritual experiences—negative and positive.
- Physical Sensitivity: prone to feeling easily drained or exhausted, lacking in stamina when compared to others'

stamina; perhaps prone to illness or insomnia; you require frequent rests or naps to recuperate and sustain.

- Sensory Sensitivity: prone to feeling overcome or overwhelmed by too much light, harsh or startling sound/music, uncomfortable textures in clothing or edibles, and/or scents that are aversive, such as detergent smells.

- Spiritual Sensitivity: prone to having powerful or vivid dreams, sensing a presence (negative and positive), being attentive to "coincidences," and/or being highly intuitive with people, animals, and nature.

If you identify with the preceding domains, you might be called a "sensitive soul," one who is challenged to assimilate with the world at large. Let's face it, the world hurts. It can be assaultive to our senses and emotions on a daily basis. Others can be selfish or aggressive. Thus, being a sensitive soul is a double-edged sword. However, the world needs more sensitive people in it. Please wear your gentleness as a badge of honor, and disallow anyone from attempting to wean the sensitivity out of you. It's hard to be human, and Earth ain't for sissies. Give yourself credit for being present. Celebrate your sensitivities, and embrace the intuitive aspect of your personhood that grants an understanding of spiritual synchronicities. You will then properly discern certain aromas and music as authentic communications, not nuisances or intrusions. This is the way of Spirit-speak.

CHAPTER 6

What Becomes a Name?

Another form of spiritual symbolism is to consider that our names may indicate our destiny. Some examples are obvious, such as Carpenter, Mason, Miller, Smith, or Ferryman. Nothing dictates or obligates anyone to become their name by trade or avocation. These names represent designations with which certain individuals became identified in their ancestral community. But it is fascinating to speculate that, for some, a spiritual correspondence has been embedded with one's surname. Other names appear peculiar in their relevance, a puzzling cryptogram after a fashion.

For example, I have noted more than one funeral home with the family name Smoot. This uncommon name intrigued me to percolate some attendant possibilities. Depending upon enunciation, Smoot can sound like "smote," one definition of which means to "strike dead." This becomes synchronous when you consider the line of work for some Smoots. Moreover, Smoot spelled backward is Tooms, which sounds the same as "tombs," which, of course, are graves or places of burial. So, in a roundabout way, it makes logical sense that Smoots should be in the funeral business.

My own name, Stillman, is significant to me personally on several counts. I have always felt that I was born in the wrong era. In particular, I have felt drawn to 1930s-era Hollywood. As a child, I was fascinated by all things Disney and the process of animation. I have also felt tied to the operations of a motion picture studio. I suspect this holds a past-life connection. Where fame is concerned, I feel as if I've "been there, done that." I have known and befriended many actors, actresses, and craftspeople who worked in motion pictures of the period. Being in their company has always felt like "old home week" to me. By the same token, I have never been impressed with anyone's wealth or celebrity; it feels as if I'm simply part of it myself. For example, I can tell if I'm being photographed to my best advantage by sensing the heat on my face from the lamps. I can "recall" the smell of motion picture equipment as it is turned on and warms up. I can "smell" the scent of recycled wardrobe and the musk of pancake makeup. Was I there? Is it real or imagined?

Interestingly, when I was born, my father worked at CBS Television in Manhattan, and I remember my mother once telling me that we were distant relatives of Ida Lupino, a movie star of the 1930s and '40s. "Stillman" was also the title given to photographers responsible for taking still pictures on movie sets that would be used to promote films in the media. I have realized my ambitions and alleged roots by researching 1930s Hollywood, which has resulted in several successful books.

As a child, I was an artistic prodigy with skills that elicited commissions of art work from adults. My first, last, and middle name are identical with that of William James Stillman (1828–1901), a prominent American artist, author, and historian. Is this a correspondence with the name, or merely coincidence? In serving people with developmental disabilities since 1987, a number of good folks have said my name is fitting. They equated my calm demeanor with the adage "still waters run deep," and found me tranquil or "a still man." In middle age, I became a professional psychic. As such, I make appearances as a "one-man show" in theaters and performing arts centers. Although I am casually known as "Bill," I use the name "William" professionally, which can be interpreted as "Will, I am." As a medium, some have said my role is to speak to deceased or "still men," befitting my name on yet another level.

In February 2017, the Internet outlet *Global News* reported that the Hebrew University of Jerusalem conducted a study that found that 40 percent of the time, strangers accurately guessed someone's name when shown photo portraits and when given four possible name choices. This isn't a bad average when you consider how we're conditioned to view others and ourselves based on how society at large correlates a name with an "identity." How often have we thought someone doesn't look like a Bob or a Beth? I have personally encountered others who appear ideally suited to their names.

One gentleman with the last name Lucky seemed to radiate goodness and glad intentions. A physician whom I consulted was regrettably named Dr. Dye. It appeared, however, that he was doing work to counteract any misperceptions of mortality associated with his name. A woman with the last name Schautz (pronounced "shouts") was perceived, by some, to be outspoken, if not abrasive, in her role as a political advocate. A firefighter with the Lafayette (Pennsylvania) Fire Company since 2007 has the surname Freeburn. A professional colleague, whose writings I admire, is named Smartt. Her associate's last name is Moody, and she has remarked that indexes list their research entries as "Smartt and Moody."

Elsewhere, former New York congressman Anthony Weiner owes his personal and professional undoing to a series of sexual indiscretions. His name is, of course, schoolyard slang for male genitalia. U.S. Congressman Rand Paul's last name sounds like *pol* as in *politician*. The first time I saw the name Reince Priebus, former Chief of Staff to President Donald Trump, I read it so quickly that I conflated it to be the word *rebus*. A rebus is a pictogram puzzle with hidden meanings to solve what it represents. Some may contend that the definition of rebus applies to Mr. Priebus's position—decoding, or interpreting, for the administration.

Usain Bolt, a Jamaican sprinter, has embodied his name for being the "fastest person ever." Bolt holds multiple world records for his extraordinary running speed. One translation of his first name is the word *beautiful*. His last name is synonymous with a rapid bolt or powerful streak of lightning and he is, indeed, lightning-fast. In motion, one might say he is like a "beautiful bolt."

One of the finest instances of people who are their name is the 1967 landmark Loving Decision, also known as *Loving v. Virginia*. Richard Loving and Mildred Jeter were an interracial couple who, in 1958, lived in Virginia, where it was illegal for people of different races to marry. That June, they made a trip to be wed in Washington, D.C., where their marriage was legal, before returning to their home in Central Point, Virginia. On July 11th, their home was raided by police at 2 a.m. who arrested them in violation of a Virginia code prohibiting interracial couples from marrying out of state and living in Virginia. Their union, it was contended, was illegal and invalid in Virginia. The Loving's one-year prison sentence was suspended when they agreed to relocate and not return as a couple for 25 years. For all intents and purposes, the Lovings were banished.

Ultimately, the Lovings were dissatisfied with this arrangement for being unable to travel to Virginia together to visit family and friends. In 1964, they engaged the American Civil Liberties Union (ACLU), which filed a motion to eliminate the Virginia Commonwealth charges against the Lovings. The Lovings' case was eventually appealed in the United States Supreme Court, where the convictions against the couple were overturned as unconstitutional, in violation of the Fourteenth Amendment's Due Process Clause and Equal Protection Clause. Additionally, the Court found the Commonwealth's marriage statutes racist and designed to reinforce white supremacy. The final ruling led to the dismantling of similarly biased laws in other southern states while giving rise to an increase in mixed-race marriages. Curiously, according to a 2012 interview with daughter Peggy, neither Richard nor Mildred ever intended to be activists; they simply wanted to live their lives peacefully. It was said the Lovings changed the country by living up to their name.

New Republic magazine's January 8, 2014, edition featured an intriguing piece by Alice Robb that further fuels the speculation that spiritual predestiny is embedded in our names. The article cites research published in the journal *Attitudes and Social Cognition* by psychologists from the State University of New York at Buffalo. The research suggests that people's names influence who we are and what we become through a phenomenon called *implicit egotism.* The concept is that subconsciously we tend to prefer people, places, and things that we associate with ourselves. This leads to an "ownership effect" in which people gravitate toward objects and even vocations that are most closely identified with self and are therefore prized and valued positively. The ownership effect, it is theorized, extends to our names and even individual letters in names.

The study looked at people who became dentists and lawyers by consulting the websites of the American Dental Association and the American Bar Association. The researchers next scanned the 1990 census looking for the four top male and female first names that shared a minimum of three letters with the two professions. They restricted their search to the nine most populous states and discovered names such as Denise, Dena, Laura, and Lauren for women, and Dennis, Denver, Lawrence, and Lance for men. Interestingly, men and women with *La* names were several times more likely to be lawyers than those with *Den* names, who became dentists. Another trial focused specifically on whether men named Dennis were more likely to become dentists as opposed to men named Jerry or Walter (the three names were ranked 39th, 40th, and 41st most common in the 1990 census). It was found that a random sampling of dentists in all 50 states, Dennis was indeed most common, ranking at 482, whereas Walter was 257, and 270 dentists were named Jerry. It's fascinating to think that the old adage "You are what you eat" could also morph into "You are what you're named."

On occasion, our names intersect with others in a mysterious manner. A complete explanation of why or how this occurs must await us in the afterlife. An example of such an improbable coincidence occurred on June 14th, 1969. Six-year-old Dennis Martin was visiting Spence Field with his family in the Great Smoky Mountains National Park. The Martins encountered another family, also named Martin, and the children of both families began a game of hide-and-seek. Dennis was last seen hiding behind some brush before inexplicably vanishing into thin air. An extensive search, ongoing for months, failed to reveal any trace of Dennis, despite the efforts of law enforcement, the FBI, and search dogs that could not pick up a scent. Hours after Dennis's disappearance, another family of hikers with the last name Key, heard a bloodcurdling scream and saw a human-like figure with something slung over one shoulder in an area six miles from Spence Field. To this day, Dennis Martin's disappearance remains unsolved.

Another incident of parallel names connecting one to another concerns Leigh Cooper, a student at North Carolina's Appalachian State University, who was abducted in September 1989 while out running. Her abductor used his vehicle to block her path and for a split moment, there was an opportunity for her escape. But when the driver flashed a pistol, Leigh felt compelled to enter the car. Her captor assaulted and raped Leigh, and threatened her life. At one point, he opened the glove compartment and she saw an envelope addressed to him. His name was Daniel

Lee. Leigh managed to safely slip away when Lee stopped for gas. Lee was apprehended shortly thereafter. During her capture, he confessed to another assault, which led authorities to discover the remains of a local woman whom Lee had raped and murdered. Lee ultimately received the death sentence in 1990 but died while incarcerated in 1997, the aftereffects of a previous brain aneurysm. Leigh Cooper died suddenly from pneumonia in December 2012 at age 43. In the intervening years, however, she had become an outspoken advocate as the survivor of a violent crime.

In my psychic work, the concept of names in rebus form is prominent. In keeping with the notion of celestial charades, word association with visuals has been one way by which Spirit communicates an approximation for a deceased loved one's name. For example, when I was shown a pile of boulders, it informed me that "rocks" equals "Rocky" or "Roxy." Donald Duck represents the name Donald. The name Art came through to me as a hard "R." This makes sense if you consider that most people wouldn't clearly enunciate the "T" in Art when pronouncing the name. It would sound more like "Arrr." In other instances, I have been shown a former acquaintance named Barry to symbolize any male with an "ry" name, such as Jerry or Gary.

Once, in the middle of a private session with a client, her maternal grandfather made his presence known and showed me a picture of President Lincoln. I thought this peculiar, wondering if the grandfather had been a Civil War buff, until my client explained that her grandfather's name was Abraham. On a walk before a psychic event, my mind was relaxed and susceptible to input. I was shown Edith Bunker from the classic sitcom *All in the Family* yelling for "Gloria," her TV daughter. When I got inside, I briefly smelled cigarettes as I walked past the bathroom. I knew to start my event by asking about a mother figure that smoked and was connected to the name Gloria who had passed. Sure enough, one person in the audience had a mother fitting that description whose name was Gloria. That Gloria would make communicative attempts on me hours before the event was in keeping with her flamboyant personality.

Just as there are spiritual communications embedded in our lives through ethereal alignments and threes, so can a name represent a broader concept. On Thanksgiving Day 2016, I was introduced to my brother's rescue cat, Ezekiel, a feisty yet playful puss with orange tiger markings. Ezekiel is an unusual, uncommon name with biblical origins. Four days later, I found the name Ezekiel spontaneously popping into my head and, a few hours later, I saw the name in print in a comic book originally published in 1946! Immediately afterward, I got a bit of good news via e-mail in which an outstanding situation was now resolved. In this case, it wasn't the significance of the repetition of the name, which is Hebrew for "God will strengthen," so much as what Ezekiel symbolized. Through a quick Google search, I discovered that in the Eastern Orthodox Church, Ezekiel is commemorated as a saint. For more than 20 years of his life, Ezekiel was a prophet who had spiritual visions and made predictions. It certainly seemed synchronous that Ezekiel was selected as the visionary to herald closure on something that had me concerned.

Have you reflected on your own name? Perhaps you were christened after someone, such as a relative, ancestor, or an individual who made an impact on your family's life. Does your life in any respect parallel that of your namesake, or are you the polar opposite? Maybe your name was chosen because of its traditional meaning or its translation in another language. The historical origins of your last name might be learned about on an ancestry website. You may be surprised to correlate your first or last name with unique, synchronous, or spiritual connotations. By the same token, your last name may be something to overcome if it risks defining you as something untoward or unbecoming, such as the names Leach, Loss, or Pigg.

You may also wish to expand this concept to include your married name. Consider whether the matrimony adjustment to your name has had an effect on your personhood beyond the obvious. Did you keep your original name, hyphenate your name, or accept your spouse's last name as your own? Has that added another layer to the realm of possibilities where spiritual relevance is concerned? It may be akin to my vision of altering relationship dynamics by the adding or taking away of purple bubbles.

For example, when I was a little boy, I was terribly alone and felt socially inept and ostracized. I wondered if there was another little boy somewhere out there who was passionate about the same things as I was, and who possibly even bore a physical resemblance to me. As it happened, I met that person in the early 1980s, about a decade beyond my yearning wish. Not only that, our last names both begin with the letter "S" and each contains the same number of letters (books have been written about numerical correspondences with letters in names). The parallels between our lives, our common interests, our experiences, and our respective families have been uncanny. My friend and I are both from a family of four boys. As children, we would have looked similar, with the same black bangs. As with many pairings, one's strengths compensates for the other's weaknesses. Beyond that, however, there have been correlations in the personalities of family members including the timing of deaths. I can only reconcile it from the perspective of something preordained.

If you have changed your name based on personal or preferential reasons, you had the benefit of selecting an identity that few of us undertake. You likely made this adjustment carefully, not recklessly, and with great thought. You may be honoring someone whom you desire to emulate or tribute. You may believe as though the name change makes you feel completely differently, defines your new personality, or validates your being. Your newly christened name may be connected to another culture, which may portend the calling to a past-life association. I have found it to be a curious thing, spiritually speaking, when people with no apparent connection to a certain heritage opt to alter their name in keeping with the culture of that heritage.

In addition to these thoughts, it may be worthwhile to explore whether your first, middle, and/or last name could be an anagram. An anagram is a word that creates other, different words when its letters are rearranged out of order. For example, "debit card" can be reworked to spell "bad credit." Indeed, some names seem to be predictors. According to anagrammer.com, the name George Bush translates to "He bugs Gore." Tom Cruise's anagram is "I'm so cuter." And Bruce Springsteen can be made to read "Creep brings tunes." My first and last name reconfigure to spell "William's all mint," or "William's mint all," which is fortuitous given my penchant to collect rare items in pristine shape and to keep my home looking as neat and new as "mint" condition.

Some names are differentiated only by the addition or deletion of one letter. Use all versions in manipulating anagrams. Other names sound alike but are spelled differently, such as Mark and Marc or Kortne and Courtney. Also take into account that you may be known by more than one name or a nickname. Play with such variations to see if it creates interesting results. If your name translates to a meaning in another language, try working with both versions. Be frivolous in your exploration, and you may just happen upon a series of congruous alliances that suggest something supreme at hand.

CHAPTER 7

The Nature of Patterns

As human beings, we have historically looked to our immediate environment for information that shapes and guides our belief systems and way of living. This includes incorporating nature, animals, and weather into global concepts that impact our daily routines. For example, you have heard the ancient adage, "Red sky at night, sailor's delight; red sky at morning, sailors take warning." (Some versions replace "sailor" with "shepherd.") Since the dawn of time, we have revered and feared aspects of nature we cannot control or understand. Certain spiritual beliefs and mythologies have given authority to the sun and the moon, or personified them with deities of their own.

This is particularly true of the Native American culture, whose spiritual beliefs connote not a religion but a lifestyle. Tribes have a spiritual leader, called shaman by those not indigenous to the culture. Spiritual rituals center upon honoring and appealing to the weather, the sun, animals, and preparation for, and closure of, hunting expeditions. There is also a strong belief that inanimate objects have spiritual qualities as well, impressed with a life force that touches all things.

Have you noticed that shapes, patterns, and color combinations found in nature have inspired the design of the fashions we wear? So, too, is this true of Native American culture. Tribal art incorporates plants, trees, flowers, and animals to symbolize aspects of life or to represent certain concepts. Like Egyptian hieroglyphics, Native American art makes use of symbols or pictograms to represent bigger concepts in minimalist presentation—the same as clairvoyant communication in Spirit-speak. A primitively rendered tortoise might symbolize longevity, whereas the Native American representation of the Universe is a large, upturned eye. The symbol for wisdom is a concentric diamond form with a dot at its center, indicating the medicine man's keen vision.

To adhere to Native American tenets is to admire the glories of nature but preserve its sanctity by leaving it untouched and undisturbed. All of nature has a profound intelligence that cares for its own while also tending to our needs. Nature is our healing ally, which commands respect and appreciation. As such, we may collaborate with the energetic patterns found naturally in outdoor environments. Allow the granite and quartz to absorb unwanted memories; permit the trees to untangle your cares and concerns with their branches; and let the cooling breeze soothe you. Whenever we become too grandiose, nature reminds us that, indeed, we do not have ultimate authority.

More than supposition, there is research to support these concepts. You've heard of sunbathing. Well how about "forest bathing"? Shinrin-yoku, which translates to "spending more time among trees," is a national health program initiated in Japan since 1982. Walking in the woods, or forest bathing, has been found to be beneficial to human health. From a psychological standpoint, walks among trees are therapeutic and naturally elevates one's mood thus alleviating depression. There are also physical benefits apart from the obvious exercise. Trees emit oils, or phytoncides, that repel insects and retard rot. But phytoncides also aide the human immune system by reducing stress and lowering both heart and blood pressure. In short, being with trees, and nature in general, is a healthy, symbiotic relationship.

Native Americans are also well aware that nature is shared, not owned, with other races. Some humans have an attitude of entitlement about land and nature when, in fact, we coexist with other beings from other realms who were here long before us. It is the elementals—entities of nature—who beckon and implore us to have greater regard for the earth. The elementals are ever present but usually dormant in winter. Some are mortal but live twice as long as humans. They are rarely seen by the human eye. When we appreciate nature, the elementals rejoice with delight in the collective kinship. It is they who contribute an energy that melds with plant life, creating growth, beauty, and sustenance. Thus, the Earth's bounty provides for all our needs through plants that nourish us or have natural medicinal properties.

Leslie Cabarga is the author of the book *Talks with Trees: A Plant Psychic's Interviews With Vegetables, Flowers and Trees*. In his book, Cabarga affirms the role of the elementals in concert with plant life, validating Native American belief systems. This occurs through his telepathic communion with a variety of vegetation. Not only does it appear apparent that live plants of every genus have emotional intelligence, they also have individualistic personalities. Much like people, some of the plants Cabarga interviews are young and vibrant, some are elderly but accommodating and wise, and others are disgruntled for how humankind has disrespected them and their ilk. For example, a lettuce registers this complaint: "It's curious to be alive and pulsing with energy but the one near you, tending you, seems to ignore this. It is not merely a matter of tending the soil, watering the 'plants' and weeding. You wouldn't just feed the baby then leave it alone in the crib until next day."

Further, Cabarga reports, plants possess an inextinguishable energy, as complete and complex a soul structure as that of human beings. The overview of their hierarchy within the social system of plants is fascinating to ponder. Cabarga gleans noteworthy annotations about how plant life interacts with a range of spiritual helpers who gently, playfully offer nourishment and encouragement to their budding and blooming charges. According to Cabarga's gatherings, there is a vast network of unseen, unspoken "behind-the-scenes" communications that transpire through unconventional means. This perspective prompted my own higher awareness.

One sunny autumn afternoon while on a meditative stroll, I became aware of the myriad patterns that appear to abound naturally. I became privy to a fleeting glimpse of a parallel dimension in which a transparent overlay was removed from my average vision, revealing the obvious: tree limbs stretched against the open sky, clouds reflecting on the water's surface, and the arrangement of petals in a delicate bloom. It was like switching a cable TV station from regular mode to high-definition to enhance all clarity. A garden bed of glorious flowers is, I now speculated, nature's equivalent of a stained-glass window. At the right angle, the sunlight illuminates the flowers' delicate veins that are just like the lead, which joins together seemingly random shards of colored glass.

After a time, Spirit inspired me with an incremental thought: "What if the pattern of fallen leaves, ripples on a pond's surface, or the arrangement of birds in flight spelled out a secret language?" It was tantalizing to consider that a muted buzz of constant patterns of communication surrounds us each day, unbeknownst to most everyone. Like the Heavenly realm, these patterns are deceptively simplistic and vastly complex. Furthermore, the patterns were not isolated but were connected, interlacing to contribute to a greater scheme. It recalled other intuitive ideas that had previously been impressed within my subconscious.

Everything has an energy pattern and a color spectrum coded especially to its unique presence. Our thoughts and emotions are constantly linking and intersecting with those of others in a grand grid of energy patterns. The grid is undetected by the human eye but is as present in our world as unseen radio waves. When you come into your own, your life takes on a different pattern and a unique rhythm. This modified pattern and rhythm grants one entrée to the grid. The awakening is really a remembering of being one with all things, including the seemingly insignificant patterns around us. Indeed, relevance abounds for the asking.

This idea aligns with the concept of *Li*, a Chinese word to describe the order of nature as reflected in its organic patterns. Consider how the rain and snow erode and reshape the earth; the route that determines the flow of water over and around pebbles and stones; and the form trees take as they sprout branches— each unique unto its own. We see what we see relative to our being, but there are active worlds of life seen only by a microscope. Thus, the micro explains the macro. The reverse is also true. The macro informs a bigger, universal understanding. As I learned, my musing on the pattern of fallen leaves, how they got there, and how plant life might orchestrate such synchronicities may be more than random.

University of Western Australia biology professor Monica Gagliano, coauthor of the 2017 book *The Language of Plants*, has found that plants communicate with one another using sound. Gagliano discovered by listening to the root systems of young corn plants that they regularly produced sounds in the range of 220Hz, which is a frequency audible to the human ear. They accomplish this by reacting to and emitting sounds via a series of clicks produced by their roots, like Morse code. It is hypothesized that such inter-flora communication is essential to the survival of plant life. But plants have also been shown to hold influence with one another through nano-mechanical oscillations on a molecular scale. Gagliano wrote, "Scientists also know that plants use volatile chemicals to communicate with each other." In some instances, plants may actually be interconnected in a vast web of communication. Such was the finding of Professor Olaf Kruse, PhD, scientific director of Germany's Bielefeld University's Center for Biotechnology. Kruse's biological research team showed that green algae not only engages in photosynthesis, it has an alternate source of energy by drawing it from other plants. "Considering that entire forests are all interconnected by networks of fungi," said Gagliano, "maybe plants are using fungi the way we use the Internet."

If, as Gagliano has stated, plants lack brains and neural tissues but do have a sophisticated calcium-based signal network similar to animals' memory processes, then do we also exchange energy with them? It gave me reason to pause when I considered something that had attracted my attention on my walks in springtime. I always wait until I get to the entrance of a wooded trail before saying prayers and reflecting in meditation. It wasn't until recently that I noticed that the plant life in the area where I began my prayer seemed to bud and bloom quicker as compared to plants on the remainder of my stroll. Indeed, I could measure the duration of my walking prayer from beginning to end; for after I concluded my meditation, the plant life was far less green and growth seemed less accelerated. I wondered if my energy in those sacred moments was imprinted on the plants I passed and if it made a difference in their reaction to me. The same holds true in our interaction with the life-sustaining liquid we all depend upon each day: water.

Are you old enough to recall the mood ring craze of the 1970s? The idea was that the translucent "stone" of the ring would change hue in accordance with one's mood. The stone is often either hollow quartz or glass filled with thermotropic liquid crystals. In short, the crystals react to temperature, in this case the body temperature of the ring-wearer, and change color in keeping with an increase or decrease in warmth. Our physiologic composition is 70 percent water and 70 percent of our world is water; it is conducive, then, that we should feel connected to, and reactive to, liquids, as is the underlying principle of the mood ring mechanics. As it happens, it's a concept similar to the late Dr. Masaru's Emoto's experiments with water crystals reacting to words and music.

Dr. Emoto passed away at age 71 in 2014, but for more than 25 years prior, he had studied water, stating, "When asking the question 'What is life?', we first need to understand water, because without water, it is impossible for there to be life or to maintain life." If you've never been without it, water, like plant life, is something easily overlooked and taken for granted. Also like the plant life that surrounds us, water appears to possess an emotional intelligence that is routinely disregarded. Dr. Emoto published his findings in his *New York Times* best-selling book *The Hidden Messages in Water*.

Comparing and contrasting tens of thousands of water crystal photographs, Dr. Emoto discovered that water reacts to positive, loving, and optimistic intentions, vibrations, and music. Interestingly enough, water also distinguishes between such sensations and those that are hateful, negative, and discordant. When exposed to unharmonious or dissonant music, such as heavy metal with crude language, the water crystals photographed appear muddy-colored and tightly concentric. But when "Yesterday" by The Beatles was played, the photograph shows a water crystal that is multi-faceted and luminous, shimmering like a diamond. Before and after pictures were also taken in conjunction with prayer ceremonies. The difference is very similar to the water crystals' exposure to assorted pieces of music. The before photos are rather dull and nondescript, but the after photos show water crystals that have blossomed into designs as intricate as snowflakes.

These experiments extended to observing how water reacts when placed in jars labeled with words such as "love" and "hate." It is an important lesson to fully comprehend as it relates to how we, as people, respond to external stimuli. The consumption of such stimuli holds great potential to positively or adversely affect our internal being across the mental-emotional, physical, and spiritual domains. This is not unlike my vision of witnessing the manner in which damaged soul energies are reshaped and restored with the loving support of wiser, compassionate allies.

In other words, because we are mostly comprised of water, what we look at, watch, and read affects us at a cellular level, beyond what we do and say. It is a concept in keeping with the aspiration to create a vessel of utmost purity for enhanced interaction with Spirit. This knowledge underscores our relationship with the great divine through our own expressive and reactive communications. Think about how language matters and words can hurt or heal. Consider how "Thank you" or "I love you" resonates within, affecting your mood and attitude, as opposed to insults and degradations. Again, there is much to be learned by broadening our perception of that which is seen and unseen in all that surrounds us.

We cohabitate with many species of birds, from finches and sparrows to pigeons, doves, and thrushes. Unless we're ornithologists, or bird watchers, we tend to pay no mind to the constant presence of birds. We know that there is instinctive logic to bird behavior and flight patterns. For example, Canadian geese know to migrate as the seasons change. They fly in V formation to break the head wind, creating a flowing draft on which to cruise. When those in the lead fatigue, others take up the slack by shifting position. These underlying rationales are lost on the casual observer but their operation upholds instinctive goose logic. So-called resident Canadian geese have no need to fly south so long as they can locate open water; in water, their bodies are insulated and they remain warm from their down feathers. Flocks of birds can seem to function as a single unit, swinging, swooping, and swaying collectively like a school of fish. After all, creatures of the land, sea, and air have their own languages, their own personalities, and their own societies. They know nothing of money, law, or politics. They are constantly connected to the Source.

What if, I wondered, how birds perch or fly is relevant to us as well? Is there a cryptic code embedded in how they appear to us in the given moment we observe them? It could be like Braille or an entirely foreign language awaiting our translation. It seemed like a random prospect until I happened upon a YouTube video of birds on telephone lines, titled "Birds on Wires." According to the video description:

> One morning while reading a newspaper, Jarbas Agnelli saw a photograph of birds on an electric wire. He cut out the photo and was inspired to make a song using the exact location of the birds as musical notes. He was curious to hear what melody the birds created. He sent the music to the photographer, Paulo Pinto, who told his editor, who told a reporter, and the story ended up as

an interview in the newspaper. It ended up Winner of the YouTube Play Guggenheim Biennial Festival.

"Birds on Wires" is magically simplistic in its rhythm and melody. Although it may not be an original idea, it is one that reminds us of the mystical intersection between the existence of nature, quietly going about its business, despite the human barrage of egocentric drives, desires, and distractions.

Consider this when reflecting on your own relationship with nature and a receptivity for playing celestial charades. Perhaps you observed that some positive people have good "relationships" with their automobiles and have a knack for getting devices or appliances to work for them. Contrast this with the person for whom the same devices malfunction in their hands. It is probable that you know someone who is a "glass half empty" pessimist. This person may be easily stressed, has lots of nervous energy, and is frequently irritable and opinionated. Perhaps this person practically lives on diet soda and junk food. It may be that he or she grapples with toxic vices, or is always the epicenter of real or imagined controversy. Now, think on the person who is pleasant and optimistic. This person's lifestyle includes a diet of consuming water, fruits and vegetables, and lean proteins. He or she is likely to be very open-minded, gracious, and accepting. It is this dichotomy in our humanity that most often separates the pragmatist from the dreamer, and the cynic from the believer.

Would you believe that patterns in nature have also given rise to our present, and evolving, technology such as cell phones? The deeper I delved, the more apparent it became that we are surrounded by natural elements placed here by intelligent design. The very essences of life permeate all of nature, making order out of seeming disorder. *Fractals* is the term coined by mathematician Benoit Mandlebrot in 1975 to correlate theoretical fractional dimension to geometric patterns in nature. It builds on the concept of self-similarity, which is something that looks like the whole even when you examine a part. For instance, the pattern of branches on a tree that continue to spread out in similar patterns repeated throughout the tree. Think of it as being like the book jacket you've seen in which the cover art depicts someone holding the same book you are, yourself, holding. Thus, the illustration theoretically repeats itself into infinity.

In nature, the concept of self-similarity is found in everything from an intricate spider web to a spiraling nautilus shell to the veins and capillaries in the human circulatory system. Even when examined under microscopic magnification, the pattern begets itself the same as the infinity picture. This can be corresponded to mathematical concepts using fractals. Like kaleidoscope patterns that that expand in perpetuity, mathematical iterations of endlessly repeating calculations have advanced our technology. Solutions have been derived from the natural selection of embedded forms that were always there but were, essentially, invisible. For example, fractals shaped like snowflakes are the building blocks of radio-reception antennae, antennas used in cell phones, and in emerging, complex telecommunications.

It is heartening to acknowledge that we are created to complement the patterns found in nature, from the vibrational frequencies of plants to the reactions of water to the instinctive habits of untamed creatures. It is a mystical embodiment of synchronicity that affects each of us throughout our everyday lives. The proper response is to accept the whole of nature as a spiritual ally; our interactive relationship with nature is our birthright, if we choose to exercise free will. It would seem, however, that we have only just begun to scratch the surface of uncovering the depths of that relationship, and the secrets which may be revealed.

CHAPTER 8

Dreamland

Recently Kate, a longtime client, came to me for a psychic reading. I discerned that she was undergoing a transition in her life. It looked as though she would be slowly delegating and phasing out job responsibilities. Simultaneously, it seemed as though she would be exploring her personal intuition. Midway through the session, Kate's deceased mother came through, indicating her eventual loss of speech. The mother further validated her presence by wearing a nightgown, coughing, and thanking her daughter for keeping her feet warm. Kate affirmed that this description was accurate: Her mother coughed quite a bit, lived in her nightgown, and always complained of cold feet. The mother also communicated that she, too, had an interest in all things mystical. The difference was that Kate was free to indulge this intrigue while her mother read about horoscopes and dreams on the sly. The mother encouraged Kate where unlimited possibilities were concerned.

As a result of this information, Kate felt comforted and inspired to develop her intuitive skills, but she required some clarity. Kate said that she had been experiencing a series of recurring dreams that had her perplexed. Her interpretation was that these dreams were attempts to stymie her. In one repeating scenario, she was frustrated by trying to open a large jar of maraschino cherries. Kate could unscrew the lid but couldn't break through the protective seal. Kate associated maraschino cherries with cocktails and was worried that it was a harbinger of alcoholism.

In other dreams, Kate was on a college campus but always got lost; was confused about the schedule or locker combination; couldn't find her classroom; or was so late for class that she was uncomfortable entering the room. Such circumstances led to her fear of flunking for missing most of the semester. (This was familiar to me, as I once had many dreams about being in university classrooms and libraries.) Kate had similar dreams about being in airports and missing her flight, getting the flight schedule mixed up, and being unable to find the correct gate. With no alternate flight available, Kate was regularly stranded at the airport.

Kate also had dreams about bodies of water, such as being on a vacation beach but unable to reach the ocean. She too had visions of a rapidly moving river with lots of people, animals, and things rushing past her. But when Kate would go near the water, it always dried up. For the occasions when she was on the water, Kate found her boat unwieldy. It would turn sideways, overcome by the current, or there would be such a congestion of boats that Kate couldn't navigate properly. In these dreams, Kate noted, the water was always fast moving but not dangerously so.

I explained my interpretation of the dreams to Kate. Simply distilled, they formed a mantra: Get out of your own way and let the Universe work with you. As Kate was at a crossroads, she was feeling a lot of anxiety by doubting her own abilities. As soon as she spoke of cherries, I immediately thought of "life is a bowl of cherries." This is a euphemism meaning life is great, fun, and carefree. She was entitled to the jar of cherries but was blocking herself from accessing what they represented by creating the unbreakable seal.

Similarly, the college campus symbolized elevated education and higher learning. Again, Kate was blocking herself from participating by creating the disorientation that disallowed her from being included. The airport literally represented accelerated advancement. But, again, Kate's fears were disallowing her from taking flight. I next explained that the closest earthly approximation to being in Spirit once again was the buoyancy of being suspended in water. Kate's efforts to attain this lightness of being evaporated when she came too close, though she could see others going with the flow. Simply put, Kate was allowing herself to be a victim.

Once she was granted this perspective, Kate had an *Aha!* moment. She realized that she was ready and prepared to move forward. Furthermore, her adolescent, but streetwise, Spirit Guide came forward and volunteered to be Kate's hall monitor by escorting her safely to the next class. Kate validated this by saying that she felt her Spirit Guide was young and "sassy." We concluded the session feeling optimistic that Kate was now empowered to move ahead.

Dreams are a common vehicle by which Spirit may communicate to us. We are kept informed about the individuality of our human experience in dreams that are uniquely our own. We are relaxed in slumber's repose and susceptible to divine infusion within our subconscious. We've been conditioned since infancy that anything can happen in dreams. This understanding makes the concept of dreaming palatable. The impossible becomes plausible because it is a figment of our imagination. Or is it? The veil between worlds is thinnest when we enter the realm of dreams, in which all things are possible.

Just as Spirit may commune with us using symbolic shorthand in real time, so may we receive similar information in dreams. But the advantage to receiving this information in dreams is the sensation of real time. We are asleep, yet "awake" and lucid as participants or observers. Furthermore, we may experience people, places, and things that are otherworldly. We may levitate, defying gravity. We may breathe underwater. We may find ourselves transformed. In short, the rules of physics don't apply and mythologies coexist within our frame of reference. Sleep is Spirit's way of mandating meditation from us each day. Dreams are a celestial ritual that commands our attention. In brief, we are a captive audience.

Dreams provide us with a forum for experiencing pure fantasy, reuniting with deceased loved ones, psychological venting, and problem-solving opportunities. Recurring nightmares are not necessarily premonitions of tragedy or portents of prophecy. Rather, repetitious nightmares may be like the song that loops repeatedly and unwillingly in one's consciousness. In certain instances, you, yourself, may be symbolized by the very threat of danger you find so exhausting to evade. You can gain greater control of your dreams by consciously setting boundaries and intentions before bedtime. In this manner, I have adjusted how I experience the now-rare nightmare dream. Instead of being an active participant, I am now merely an observer, a bystander watching from the sidelines of a movie set as the action plays out before me. I have also achieved a degree of consciousness in such dreams by emphatically renouncing any nefarious character, and rebuking it with authority. If you are so plagued, try asserting yourself and reclaiming control in this way.

Premonitions may come to us in dreams as harbingers of what is to come. I recall, on two distinct occasions in my early childhood, having dreams in which I picked coins out of the grass on my front lawn. The very next day, I did just that, wondering how in the world all that loose change got scattered across the grass. Oddly, this happened not in the same home, but in two separate locations.

Premonitory dreams may also present merely the possibility to inform us of one future scenario. This is not necessarily what will come to pass, but is like viewing the trajectory of a parallel timeline, much like how Ebenezer Scrooge was shown his possible future if he did not make amendments to his current life. Thus, the predictions in dreams might be projections of alternative possibilities. The perfect example of this kind of premonition occurred to me in a "waking dream," or a standing vision that I perceived during a psychic reading.

During the session with my client, I sensed an impending birthday. After some thought, it dawned on my client that her daughter was expecting a granddaughter to be born imminently. I next felt as if the baby would be born on a "special day." We assumed that the special day would be on or about Christmas, such as December 24th or 25th, or even New Year's Eve or New Year's Day. When the baby wasn't delivered until January 17th, 2017, my client and I were perplexed. Unbeknownst to us, however, this was indeed a powerful and meaningful date.

As it is recorded in spiritual thought, January 17th, 2017, is an energetic gateway. This date initiates the Divinity Gate, which will remain "open" until 2021. As the gate opens, a new frequency of light energy pours into the world. The energy is intended to call forth changes that will result in the creation of the "Golden Age" of *prophecy*. Legends of otherworldly communities such as Shangri La, Utopia, New Jerusalem, and Shamballah speak of this Golden Age. As such, January 17, 2017, signifies the beginning process of creating the new world order.

And that is the beauty of how the Universe works. The prediction that my client's granddaughter would be born on a "special day" remained true and valid. However, the circumstances transpired differently from the way it was interpreted or expected to occur. This is an important lesson to consider so that none of us becomes overly preoccupied with dreams that we believe portend of future danger or disaster. Oftentimes, we may feel an insistent urge to forewarn others of the impending doom that never comes to pass. It could well be that we misunderstood or misinterpreted the meaning of the dream's symbolisms.

Dreams can be extraordinary vehicles for processing snippets of past lifetimes as well as parallel or alternate time lines. Often, unexplainable or irrational fears and phobias can be attributed to traumatic residue from a past life experience. That is, the traumatic event is so powerful, it likely culminated in death. Not only this, the trauma has imprinted on the very composition of the soul. This subsequently creates a cellular memory when we take human form. This is no different from how post-traumatic stress disorder survivors have physical and mental-emotional symptoms triggered by memories, scents, environments, and so on. In the new lifetime, traces of the tragedy from a previous existence are carried over. It is logical that fragments of memory would be vented using dreams as the psychological outlet.

For instance, when giving a psychic reading to a client, I intuited that her boyfriend was petrified of flying. She acknowledged this and said it extended to his occasional nightmares. It had also hampered their vacation plans more than once. I explained that his phobia was linked to his death in a past life. What I saw was that he had been a World War II pilot who was shot down in combat and perished in a fiery crash. My client needed to decide whether or not to share this information with her boyfriend, but she did acknowledge that he was a history buff and had a knack for identifying World War II aircraft, which seemingly validated my vision.

In this and similar cases, a past life regression may be recommended in order to resolve what cannot be reconciled by traditional means of psychological treatment. In a past life regression, a licensed hypnotherapist will gently guide the client into a relaxed state that is open and susceptible, not unlike a trance or dream state. The therapist may then delicately probe, respectfully following the client's lead. The therapist should refrain from leading the client into reliving a traumatic event in its entirety, and should provide calming assurances for knowing "that was in the past" if the client should become emotional.

Speaking for myself, I recall a recurring dream in my childhood in which I was "older" or presented as an adult. In the dream, there were others gathered around me inspecting a serious injury that I received in battle. I can still remember the sensation of repulsion as I looked down at my leg to see a huge flap of skin gashed open to expose the veined layer of fat underneath. Knowing what I know now, I strongly suspect this had a past life connection. Thankfully, the nightmare dissipated over time as I outgrew it.

Dreams can serve as portals into alternate realities. There is a theory that our reality is one of several realities that coincide with one another in parallel time lines. On occasion, those time lines may overlap in dreams, providing us a glimpse into another, but similar, realm. Sometimes, snatches of memories from the parallel time lines are recollected by many people and not just individuals. From our dream state, we retain what we believe to be fact as experienced in a separate trajectory. This creates confusion in the "real" world in which the majority must function. These misremembrances are called false memories by psychologists, except in these instances the false memories are *shared* memories. How it is possible that scores of people unknown to one another swear they remember something that never happened? One explanation is that in our dreams there is a place in which many of us gather and connect in a like-minded community.

Parapsychologists, or those who study superhuman mental faculties, call these shared experiences "The Mandela Effect," a term coined by paranormal author and researcher Fiona Broome. (You are not alone if—after the chapter about names—you associated Ms. Broome's surname with a witch's mode of flight!) The Mandela Effect is so named because of the multitude of individuals, including Ms. Broome, who recall learning of human rights activist Nelson Mandela's death while imprisoned in the 1980s, and remember viewing it on television at the time. The trouble is, Mr. Mandela died in 2013!

Other examples of this phenomenon include many people who staunchly insist that the Berenstain Bears, longtime children's book characters, were originally the *Berenstein* Bears. As it happens, however, the Berenstein Bears never existed. The Berenstain Bears debuted in 1962 and have only ever been referred to as such. Other popular examples of such slightly off-kilter historical revisions are that comedian Sinbad starred as a genie in a 1980s fantasy film titled *Shazaam* or that *The Wizard of Oz* ends with a shot panning away from Dorothy to reveal she is either still wearing the ruby slippers or they are safely tucked away under her bed—none of which actually happened.

In the realm of cryptozoology (the study of unknown creatures), a famous Mandela Effect is that of the antique photograph that dozens, if not hundreds, of people recall seeing—myself included. The picture documents a pterodactyl that has been killed by Civil War–era soldiers or early 1900s settlers. In it, the improbable creature is either held by the gentlemen for size ratio or nailed to the side of a barn to display its wingspan. (This is not to be confused with the several fakes that have been Photoshopped as "answers" to efforts to locate the photo in question.) I am perplexed as to why this picture has been so challenging to locate, as I remember seeing it in a book from my junior high school library. I still see the red jacket of the book cover with a line drawing of, among other things, a pterodactyl. I know this is not my imagination because a gentleman from our church appeared in one of the book's pictures, examining an unusually large chunk of ice that fell from the sky. But I now wonder if I were to locate a copy of the book, if the pterodactyl picture would be mysteriously missing.

I also remember a childhood dream in which I entered the closet in my bedroom, except it wasn't mine. It was the same size and shape but someone else's things were in it. As I looked up at the shelf above the clothes rack, I saw a large-format softcover children's book. I distinctly recall the rather somber grays and browns of the cover painting, and thought it odd that a children's book cover would be so muted instead of vibrantly colorful. Sure enough, about a decade later, I came upon a copy of the exact same book, although I had seen it in a dream many years before I was aware of its existence—at least in this lifetime.

Perhaps you share one of the preceding experiences. Consider if it may be the remnant of a dream or some other mystical encounter. Also consider if it is one avenue by which Spirit is calling to you.

The concept of "dream" may also extend to include daydreaming and wishful thinking. Never dismiss the opportunity to daydream. When we daydream, we are only half aware of being present. It is an in-between sensation akin to déjà vu. Daydreams are one method by which Spirit communicates in order to impress inspiration within us. We should all allow ourselves to daydream and indulge in a rich fantasy life about unlimited possibilities that await us. In other words, don't wait until your birthday to blow out a candle and make a wish for dreams to come true. Wishes become intentions with the energy of effort!

From a scientific perspective, the purpose of dreaming is the source of ongoing research. The hows and the whys of dreaming remain much a mystery. In its April 10, 2017, online edition, *Nature*

Neuroscience published a study about the state of consciousness while dreaming. The study asserted that while awake our consciousness never dims, but upon awakening from dreaming, we may either recall our dreams or be completely unable to remember anything. (Some people swear they don't dream at all!) Dreaming has historically been associated with REM, or rapid eye-movement, sleep during which high-frequency brain activity occurs. But dreaming also occurs in non-REM sleep as well, which is marked by low-frequency brain activity. The study looked at the differences between dreaming during the two states of sleep.

The new findings discovered that an area at the back of the skull increases in low-frequency activity during sleep in which dreaming does not take place. This region of the brain is associated with recalling specific information about experiences. However, during dreams, the low-frequency activity in this region gives way to high-frequency activity. The high-frequency activity appears to then expand its reach beyond this area, extending to parts of the brain that deal with encoding and memories. It seems that the usual low-frequency mode blocks us from experiences we would recall as dreams. (My spiritual interpretation for this "amnesia" of sorts will be explained before this chapter concludes.)

When the brain is in high-frequency mode, dreams are similar to how our consciousness functions when awake, such as holding a dream conversation in which someone's speech and mouth movements are synchronized. The takeaway, as the study's researchers state, is that "dreaming may constitute a valuable model for the study of consciousness with implications beyond sleep."

Countless volumes have been written about the relevance of dreams and how to properly interpret their secret symbolisms. You may do well to avail yourself of a fluent understanding of such, particularly if you are susceptible to premonitory dreams. Remember: In addition to serving other functions, dreams are one form of Spirit-speak. It may be that certain dreams are not to be taken so literally but should be decoded in terms of any embedded symbols that may or may not be relevant. Once again, not everything is *something*.

Our dreams can be a portal to the afterworld and true reality. Thus, life is a dream your soul has in human form. Our physical death is a permanent dream from which there is no awakening because it is the new reality. Our most vivid dreams occur when our present reality intersects with the spiritual reality. This creates a temporary enclave in which reunions transpire. If you've ever had a dream in which you spent time with a deceased loved one, you may have awakened emotional and weepy. The dream you experienced was so lifelike it was just as if that person never left you. Your beloved grandfather, for instance, probably looked happy and healthy and youthful, about 30 years old. You might remember that it seemed you both communicated many things, although you will likely not recollect much of what got exchanged between you. It's also probable that neither one of you actually spoke, but felt and sensed information telepathically. Such dreams are uncommon and tend to occur when we require comfort or consoling. This type of vivid dream is called a *visitation*.

My mother passed away in her late 60s. We had been estranged for decades and had little to no communication. She forfeited much in her life for feeling entitled, and it strained her relationship with her four sons. I was aware that she lived out of state but knew little else. I got information in bits and pieces from a brother, who was getting his information from my mother's neighbor. When she died, she was the last person from whom I expected to have a visitation dream. But, sure enough, a visitation did occur several years after she crossed over. In the dream, she was a young woman who was paying me a visit at the home in which I currently reside.

She was accompanied by an older man, who I understood to be her father. She was excited to show me her new baby, a daughter which she carried lovingly, bundled in her arms. When I peeked at the infant, it was obvious the little girl had Down syndrome.

When I awoke, the relevance of the dream was plain to me. I felt it was as if my mother's soul had presented to me for my approval a next-life scenario she was contemplating. My mother never knew or met her biological father during her physical lifetime. But in the dream, she showed me that she had a positive, supportive union with her father. It felt as though the baby was born out of wedlock, so the reinforcement of this father figure would be essential to my mother's ability to understand what a male could contribute to the father-child relationship. Who knows—that dynamic could have altered the course of her own life had that influence been present. Likewise, my mother had always wished for a girl. Now she had her wish, although this baby would have special needs that would require my mother's unselfish, unconditional commitment. I thought it the perfect scenario for my mother to rectify the errors of her lifetime in a proactive, responsible manner. Suffice it to say, I approved of her choice. You may have also experienced this form of resolution during a dream state. If so, hopefully it granted you spiritual closure by responding to outstanding or unanswered questions.

Visitation dreams can also serve as an opportunity to connect with one or more Spirit Guides. I suspect this happens more frequently than what most of us remember. A dream I had in mid-February 2005 was recorded as simply "I'm in a familiar space used for problem-solving." The operative word here is *familiar*, connoting a homecoming of sorts. This scenario resonated most clearly in another dream the year before:

> Awakened shortly after midnight after having had an amazing, inspirational and vivid dream. I was in a space with a male mentor (Frank?) who gently urged, coaxed, and cajoled me to expand myself through thoughts, words, music and motion to create a constant, moving colorful fantasy-scape, all of my own doing. The message was Thought = Form, and it all became real as I imagined and sang it with him presiding— a constant morphing of fantasy images. I no longer restrained myself, and once I abandoned my self-consciousness and got into a rhythm that picked up momentum, anything was possible! I had such untapped potential that he helped me to realize in his patience;

and he celebrated it with me as I went along! It looked as spontaneous and fast-paced as a scene from *Who Framed Roger Rabbit?* set to the bass line from Stone Temple Pilot's song "Even Flow."

When our consciousness splinters from the physical and takes on a dynamic all its own, we may define it as prayer, meditation, vision, or dream. Occasionally, complex spiritual concepts get communicated in our dreams that we ordinarily would not comprehend in real time. For example, on January 2, 2003, I recorded: "Had a dream in the middle of the night; couldn't recall details with any clarity but it had something to do with explaining the dying process and what we experience in death and afterwards. I wonder if my request for mentorship hasn't been answered and that it is all occurring during sleep."

Where this amnesia is concerned, take heart. We are not supposed to recall certain dreams, as they are encrypted with a code intended solely for the soul's comprehension. It is for this reason that I believe scientific studies, such as that previously mentioned in *Nature Neuroscience*, will ultimately be hindered moving forward. We can only go so far before we risk messing with Spirit's schematics. I suspect there are strategically placed roadblocks and benign booby-traps to derail us from uncovering too much information that explains why dreaming is essential to our very being.

Because we exist in a dimension of such heavy density, our lives resemble bad editing assembled by an amateur Spielberg wannabe. As such, key pieces of information have been embedded within us. These "triggers" function like road signs such as "Detour," "Stop," "Caution," and so on. The signs will surface at the appropriate times or will, more likely, manifest in dreams. It is at the soul level that the information is translated and retained for future use in a manner that will be understood by us all once we cross into the Spirit realm.

CHAPTER 9

Autism, Dementia, and Mental Illness

Star Trek proclaims that space is the final frontier but perhaps it is *inner* space, and not outer space, that remains to be explored, charted, and settled. Reality is a matter of individual perception. It is based upon our ability to express, receive, and perceive information filtered through the human body. But it is the soul that animates the body. Soul energy is infused throughout the cellular and molecular structure of our entire being. Absent the soul's integration, the body ceases to function. This is the difference between perceiving the brain as several pounds of tissue or a functioning organ. This is the difference between life and death.

When we are infants, it is natural for us to gurgle and coo and make efforts at verbalizations. To the onlooker, it may all appear to be meaningless gibberish. But the wise parent reinforces the gibberish by repeating the proper pronunciation and pairing it with a visual object. In this manner, the infant begins to correlate "ba, ba, ba . . ." with the tangible red ball that his mother holds while saying, "ball." How, then, does one begin the process of correlating the *intangible* with correct terminology?

It is generally agreed in the metaphysical community that children are naturally inclined to psychic experiences. This is because they are chronologically closest to the experience of having been souls in the Heavenly realm. Thus, their intuition tends to be heightened and they are generally without the societal filters that come with maturity. Such filters disallow one from perceiving what the human brain determines to be illogical and irrational. As has been noted, there is no need for verbal speech in Heaven because thought and emotion are communicated telepathically. And so the cumbersome process of language acquisition—both expressive and receptive—must begin anew for infants and toddlers in the physical world. This is further complicated when one has a speech delay due to developmental differences or autism.

The manner in which individuals with autism may communicate using symbols and icons was previously discussed. Approximately half of all autistics are not wired for speech, meaning they are essentially mute. Those unaffected are verbally articulate wheras others severely compromised speak the foreign tongue known as "gibberish." Gibberish can be unintelligible or it can present itself as echolalia. Echolalia is the verbal but seemingly purposeless recitation or "echoing" of a word, phrase, or vocalization. The communication of echolalia can seem quite earnest in the individual's desire to convey its message. In other instances, the echolalia is paired with repetitive movement that appears joyful in its expression. Does echolalia equal mantra?

On the other hand, what if gibberish really is just that—gibberish? Then, one interpretation is that the jabbering is an external smokescreen for the authentic and true communication, which is clear and fluent spiritual telepathy. In this manner, the gibberish is like car exhaust. The hazy, smoky exhaust is evidence that a car is operating but you wouldn't suggest that it is the exhaust that propels the car; it's simply a byproduct of the greater action. This is analogous to how repetitive, ritualistic tribal ceremonies aren't as much about the dance or the recitations; those activities are the merely the vehicle for accessing a state of heightened consciousness. The question remaining becomes: Is the physical act of gibberish a divine veil to conceal something greater from being deciphered for being misinterpreted and dismissed as "nonsense"?

There are commonalities between the nonsensical vocalizations of the autistic and the seemingly random rambling of those whose reality is also comprised. Gibberish may be symptomatic of those affected by stroke or dementia. And, curiously, a condition associated with echolalia is aphasia, which is the impairment of speech and language comprehension. Aphasia is also commonplace in those whose neurology is compromised by stroke or dementia. However, the physiological damage to the brain may actually be the vehicle of transition to another plane of mental reality. What is conventionally considered a deteriorating insult to the brain could be the avenue to higher thought expressed in verbal hieroglyphics.

In one videotaped example of an elderly woman with aphasia, her interviewer asks that she repeat certain words. When the interviewer says "baseball," the woman replies with repetitious gibberish. But upon closer inspection, what the woman says sounds like "babe roose." It is entirely probable that the woman correlated baseball with Babe Ruth, the best known player of her era. This is also reminiscent of the autistic child that receives a failing mark for misidentifying the photograph of a suburban residence as "bird" instead of "house." Drawn to detail, he was distracted by the sparrow perched on telephone wires in the same picture. In both cases, the tested individuals did not respond with the correct response as qualified by the surveyor. Because each individual's neurology is considered pathology, they are easily dismissed. However, neither answer is incorrect and both are accurate observations.

In her *Psychology Today* essay about her mother's dementia, Dr. Jeanne Murray Walker advocated looking beneath the surface of gibberish. She wrote, "I began paying closer attention to what Mother said. I started accepting, as a matter of faith that what she said could be made sense of as references not to the present but to the past. I believed that might be happening not just once in a while, but a lot of the time, even when she sounded really unhinged." Murray Walker concludes that caretaking became less one-sided, more understandable, when she interpreted her mother's gibberish in the context of her history. It is intriguing to speculate on one's susceptibility as the recipient of unconventional information. Not everyone develops dementia. Is it a protective, psychological safeguard or is the information gently impressed and implanted from a Higher Source?

My soulmate in this lifetime was my father's mother. My grandmother and I were 50 years apart when I was born. We remained virtually inseparable until she passed away another 50 years on. Toward the end of her widowed life, she required greater assistance and moved from her home of 30 years into an eldercare setting. This was a major life change and, for the first time ever, she seemed helpless and lonely. I visited often and we talked on the phone regularly. She told me offhandedly that she was awakening to music each morning. There was an intercom in the hallway just outside her room and we thought it might be the source. But when she called the office, she was told that the intercom was used for announcements only.

The music persisted so I asked her if she could recall the songs. When she had difficulty doing so, I asked her to keep paper and pen on her nightstand to jot down her memories before they faded. This she did dutifully, passing her notes along to me at each visit. Some of her notations were song titles; others were several stanzas of lyrics. Interestingly, virtually none were repeats. She usually awakened to different songs each morning. The songs included "The Old Gray Mare," "Jeannie with the Light Brown Hair," "Camptown Races," and "Let Me Call You Sweetheart." None of it was unpleasant or intrusive, and it endured for several weeks.

A scientific explanation for my grandmother's experience is the psychological accommodation of the subconscious mind. An alteration in brain chemistry tripped ancient memories, marking the beginning of the end as she developed dementia. (Musical aptitude is rarely diminished with dementia; its powers of retention endure until the last.) But, curiously, all of the songs my grandmother identified were of a carefree, bygone era that harkened back to her childhood. A spiritual explanation is that my deceased grandfather was responsible for providing the comforting music to soothe my grandmother and ease her transition in a strange environment.

A neighbor of mine recently made the heartbreaking decision to place her husband out of home in the dementia unit of an assisted-living facility. Fortunately, he has adjusted well. Curiously, though, for him time doubles back on itself. He introduces her as his deceased brother Bob and when he speaks of going home, it is to his childhood home. My friend has noticed that many of her husband's unitmates speak to one other in a mysterious language only they seem to understand.

In addition to my own observations in nursing homes and Alzheimer's wards, I consulted a Certified Dementia Practitioner to discover any professional concurrence with my metaphysical speculations. In reply to my question about common themes of discussion in people with dementia, the practitioner was quick to respond. Without hesitation, she said the number-one topic across any number of locations centered on individuals' mothers. "I'm waiting for my mother" or "Have you seen my mother?" were commonly communicated. It seems that in an enhanced state of vulnerability, people are seeking the maternal protection they enjoyed in childhood, which also corresponds to happy memories. Comforting music, especially songs their mother may have once sung, usually serves to contain their anxiety. I could imagine that this collective outreach to "mother" would be reciprocated somehow, someway, by a loving spiritual presence in the manner I believe my own grandmother was comforted.

I also ventured a question about the mysteries of "gibberish." I wanted to know if, like my neighbor, the practitioner had seen people talking nonsensically to one another and yet appear to *understand* one another. This understanding might be demonstrated by an emotional reaction, such as shared laughter or rising together to attend an activity. Yes, the practitioner answered, this occurs often but always *one-on-one*. It can be either pleasant or unpleasant. When it is unpleasant, it happens between two men or a man and a woman; but when it is a pleasant interaction, it is always between two women. The conversation is not 100 percent unintelligible speech,

I was told, but a mixture of gibberish and understandable words such that the emotional intent gets conveyed. I wondered if this blending of gibberish and words was similar to the "car exhaust" paradigm of which I spoke relative to autism. That is to say, does the new, blended language really serve as a façade for the *true* language, which is telepathy made possible by an altered state of consciousness? If so, it would certainly be in keeping with the concept of entrainment as well as Spirit-speak.

One common language problem of those with dementia is the loss of speech altogether. People who don't talk, such as those with autism, or who lose speech gradually, such as those with dementia, become immersed in a form of perpetual meditation. Expansive amounts of time are spent in silence and, ostensibly, thought. This is akin to those of great spiritual devotion who deliberately enter into protracted periods of solitude: the nun, the monk, the yogi, the priest, the rabbi, or the guru. An altered state of consciousness is the desired outcome of the perpetual meditation enacted by holy persons. The deeper they descend into the meditation, the more their brain shifts its orientation from physical awareness to aesthetic awareness. In brief, it is about plugging in spiritually. These contentions are backed by research about the effect of prayer on the human brain.

Dr. Robert Cloninger, of St. Louis's Washington University Medical School, invented the self-transcendence scale, in part, to measure spirituality. It is based upon three components: self-forgetfulness, transpersonal identification, and mysticism. All three measurements crosswalk to traits of many individuals with dementia and autism. *Self-forgetfulness* is losing track of time and place and becoming absorbed in an utter lack of self-consciousness. Think of how easily one can lose sense of date and time in eldercare settings, or how date and time are superfluous to those with autism existing in the "now." *Transpersonal identification* is a sense of connectedness with all things in the universe, animate and inanimate, including attachments to certain people, animals, and nature. *Mysticism* is an openness to things that can't be explained by science.

There appears to be a correlation among these three components and how those who mediate may focus on a word, a sound, or an image. Also consider the musical elations achieved through Gregorian chant or the rhythmic ecstasies of the Sufi dervishes in Turkey and some African tribes. The outcome of the repetition is an altered state of consciousness, an enhancement of personal or group spiritual connectivity. Likewise, Dr. Cloninger's self-transcendence scale dovetails with the repetitive movements or vocalizations of those with autism and dementia. It is not uncommon for persons in either of these two groups to appear absorbed in repeating the same thing without seeming care or concern for time. The difference is that when those individuals similarly perseverate, it is viewed as clinical pathology instead of spiritually symptomatic.

Another trait of people with dementia is the tendency to use metaphors to convey concepts they otherwise cannot communicate. In my work as a psychic medium, there are spiritual concepts to which I am privy that are challenging to articulate. Some of us may have had similar experiences in dreams. We know we experienced something "big," but putting it into words seems impossible. So intrinsic are these concepts to their native culture that they defy language. It is akin to pronouncing the sound a noise makes using words instead of imitation. This is not unlike the reports of Dr. Michael Newton's subjects under hypnotic regression, as documented in Dr. Newton's books *Journey of Souls* and *Destiny of Souls*.

Newton tranced his patients into a hypnotic stage *between* past lives, as souls in the Heavenly realm. Newton then was able to gather details about the afterlife and draw parallels in the consistency of information from people unknown to one another.

It was not uncommon for those individuals to halt and block and confess to being unable to describe certain aspects of their observations. There were simply no terms in human language to define it. If my neurology was comprised, and I was tasked with verbally interpreting concepts, sensations, and visuals beyond my comprehension, it would probably sound like gibberish. Is this the experience of those who straddle both worlds naturally, as in autism, or by happenstance, as in those with dementia or even mental illness?

As in autism and dementia, schizophrenia, or "splitting of the mind," can include echolalia among its symptoms. This manifests in seemingly disconnected words or phrases that appear to hold no meaning but are asserted by the individual as matter of fact. Another feature is delusions, which are irrational beliefs that the individual defends rigidly even when those beliefs are proven false. Common delusions involve the sensation that one is being manipulated and controlled by an outside force, or the belief that one is receiving embedded communications in code. Visual and auditory hallucinations are associated with schizophrenia such as hearing sounds or authoritative voices. Catatonia, or an unresponsive stupor, is also symptomatic of schizophrenia. An argument could be made for a correspondence between schizophrenic catatonia and the mutism of autistics and those with dementia. Without the ability to accurately describe or express what occurs in these states of solitude, we may only speculate as to what certain individuals experience. One wonders if these persons are privy to a realm that outwardly presents as pathology to the unadmitted.

Schizophrenic delusions can lead to paranoia. Oftentimes, people with schizophrenia believe they are overhearing people's thoughts criticizing or conspiring against them. We know these are delusions because the people in question deny the allegations are true. But if someone's psychology is fractured or fragile, could there a grain of authenticity in what he or she is tuning in on? It is not unlike the classic *Twilight Zone* episode in which actor Dick York (Darrin from *Bewitched*) unexpectedly acquires the temporary ability to detect others' private thoughts. Outwardly, people appear to be civil and complacent, but their internal monologues, as "heard" by York, reflect their true selves: plotting revenge, judgmental mentality, duplicity, or plain indifference. In short, their inner-most thinking belies what they project on the surface. Interestingly enough, this experience is a lot like how psychics work and telepathy operates.

As a psychic myself, there are many times when a client enters an appointment bubbly, smiling, and seemingly on top of the world. But as soon as we enter into the intuitive reading, I quickly discern the fatigue and loss of energy linked to depression. Sure enough, these clients confess to the turmoil in their lives that otherwise goes undetected in passing. In several cases, men, in particular, try to minimize their past, downplaying the psychological, physical, or sexual abuse perpetrated upon them in boyhood or adolescence. When one illuminates the truth, its transparency cannot harbor secrets suppressed in shame or disgrace. The liberation facilitates the healing process. As much as I am not schizophrenic, I can see the argument for drawing such parallels. In fact, when I first began to uncover my spiritual gifts, I lost a couple of friends. I suspect they were increasingly uncomfortable in thinking that I was coming unhinged based upon the mysticism I openly reported. I learned the hard way to exercise caution for when, where, and with whom to share highly sensitive information. Not everyone is open to hearing it and not everyone welcomes being the spontaneous recipient of it.

Components of schizophrenia are similar to indications for bipolar disorder. In the history of modern psychiatry, the two have often been confused and bipolar disorder was frequently misdiagnosed as schizophrenia. The alternating portions of bipolar disorder comprise depressive and manic episodes. Hence, the derivation of the term *bipolar*, meaning two opposite poles. When one is in the throes of a manic episode, the mind races faster than the body can keep up with it, resulting in nearly tongue-twisting pressured speech. This breakneck speed can transfer to the body, causing psychomotor agitation, or the need to be in constant motion, often with no specific goal. One's mood can become that of a jubilant life-of-the-party persona, bordering on silliness. It is in mania that artists, poets, and musicians discover the muse for their greatest creative outlet. One's self-esteem may also become inflated, elevating the individual to a status superior to the layperson.

In the midst of such grandiosity, someone may seem paranoid by suggesting that others are surreptitiously monitoring them. But, unlike schizophrenia, now it is because of their importance or pseudo-celebrity. The same grandiosity may propel the individual to spin tall tales about otherworldly encounters with space aliens or deceased rock stars. When countered, the individual is adamant about the veracity of their experience. To them, it is all very real.

The late actress Carrie Fisher became an outspoken advocate for her own bipolar disorder. When Fisher was interviewed by journalist Diane Sawyer in 2000, she explained that her incessant, irrational chatter was an attempt to drown out the manic fire in her brain. Fisher described mania as a world of bad judgment calls that seem like good ideas in the moment. For Fisher, hallucinatory drugs quelled her brain and appeased her desire to just feel "less." As she put it, "I died to this sanity." Going to an alternate reality was, as Fisher put it, "a very sensual experience . . . as though you could feel the back of the cool of the mood with your hand. I could see futuristic cities out the window." Fisher summarized, "Losing your mind is a terrible thing, but once it's gone, it's fine. It's completely fine because there's no part of you left that knows the rest of it is missing." The sense of disconnectedness that Fisher described is a transcendental experience commonplace to those with autism and dementia, as has been noted.

Perhaps, like a compass, points of outer and inner space converge in the center of the human soul. For some, this indicates a deficiency of outer space, or the corporeal, and a surplus of inner space, or the mystical. When this imbalance occurs, it may lead to struggles to cope and assimilate to the norm. Exposure to altered states of consciousness as a matter of course is overwhelming for distinguishing fantasy from reality. Taming and refining this gifted frequency may be insurmountable. This can lead to retreat, as in those with autism; blissful sur-render, as in those with dementia; or all-out war-fare, as in those with mental illness. Regardless, it is apparent that some of us are simply too sensitive for this world.

CHAPTER 10

Abundance and Authenticity

Abundance is the satisfaction of fulfillment. It is not wealth or material possessions. It is doing what you are. Abundance begins with the belief that being good will cause you to do good things. Achieving this requires you to employ all that you have been, all that you are presently, and all that you are becoming. The sum total of your being has practical application. You are here to use your example to serve. Conducting yourself in the spirit of goodwill benefits others as much, if not more, than yourself. It sets in motion a cycle that perpetuates abundance for all. This is the manner in which the Universe operates, if you subscribe and believe.

Belief in a Higher Power is essential. It is the distinction between attracting abundance organically and working twice as hard, and twice as long, to attain a similar outcome. Consider a topic as mundane as the weather, yet it controls our everyday lives. It holds the potential to affect us across all domains: mental-emotional, physical, and spiritual. The scientific explanation for the existence of weather is meteorological: It's all accountable to naturally occurring fluctuations in the atmosphere. Pessimists complain it's raining. Optimists counter with gratitude because the rain isn't snow. Cynics complain about overcast skies to natural catastrophes. Believers acknowledge that inclement or disastrous weather grants us appreciation for sunny skies. But *who* put it there in the first place? That is the question open to debate between believers and non-believers.

In August 2016, I purchased a children's book from the 1920s. As I was paging through it, I came upon a bookmark made of faded purple construction paper. On it, inked in careful script, was written "Love's Foot Rule." Indeed, the bookmark was designed to resemble a ruler with 12 tenets representing each inch of measurement. I assumed this was made by a young girl for a school project or personal reference. As I considered the measurement entries, I thought about how each tenet correlated to the concept of abundance. It was amazing to me that a child of the 1920s understood the building blocks of spiritual prosperity. With the aid of Spirit, I crafted my definition for each measurement. Here, then, is Love's Foot Rule and the interpretation of each measurement:

- Long-suffering: To accept the purpose in doing without for being compromised or suppressed. You may be the target of others' jealousy but sustain with grace. To tolerate ignorance, within reason, until clarity is attained. Rise above circumstances with dignity. To minimize your trials as temporary nuisances. Disallow yourself from reflecting back what others may project. To be unafraid to tell your story.

- Kind: A selfless compassion for others and a concern for all things. Measured in temperament and response. An attitude projected in emotion and words, and demonstrated in deeds. Giving with the desire to serve. Gentle, considerate, accommodating. An ability to clearly distinguish hate, injustice, and duplicity from all that is right and true.

- Free from covetousness: Releasing jealousy, shedding malcontentment, and surrendering envy of others. This includes disassociation of material possessions, fame, relationships, or situations. The deception is that these things will bring happiness or contentment. Greed is a poison when self-gratification is gained quickly and by inauthentic means. Be satisfied in knowing less is more. To embrace the material as immaterial where universal ownership is concerned.

- Humble: The absence of ego. To be unconcerned with recognition. Accepting only as much credit as is due or has been honestly earned. Disdain fame and its illusion of trappings. To acknowledge that the manner in which Spirit works doesn't come from you, it comes through you. Sometimes heroic deeds come of invisible benefactors.

- Unselfish: To give of one's self willingly, be it time or resources, without the expectation of reciprocation. To be free of judgment and without motive for personal gain. To identify and fulfill others' needs without hesitation or awaiting a prompt. To sacrifice with grace as one is so called. To serve openly without hemorrhaging one's own resources by facilitating independence instead of dependency.

- Patient: To be mindful of the space you occupy while holding fast to every unfulfilled longing in anticipation of fulfillment. Abiding with perspective that is granted by the Universe. Waiting for the moment that rings true instead of forcing an urgent agenda. Knowing to occupy yourself while biding time but not wasting it.

- Pure in thought: To allow one's heart to lead the truth. To be aware of impure thoughts but to set boundaries on your space. To halt and repel thoughts that are counterproductive and destructive. To be liberated from thoughts of harming one's self or others emotionally, physically, and spiritually. Disallowing negativity from breeching one's lexicon of mantras.

- Truth-loving: To embrace and abide by authentic conduct. Steadfast in advocacy. To uphold grace. Embody the truth with the integrity of character. To be unyielding in defense of what is right and just. To speak with authority where matters of the heart are concerned. To revel in the transparency of light that illuminates the truth.

- Endurance: To pace one's stamina in order to sustain with resiliency. To stand the test of time. Tending to mind, body, and spirit to ensure optimal well-being. To honor one's personhood across struggles and obstacles. An ability to sustain and survive with determination despite adversity. To endure in love and grace. Possessed of timeless qualities that are classic and always applicable.

- Faith: The unseen but authentic will that fortifies and finances our spirit. Trust in the knowledge that all will ultimately be reconciled. Faith is the strength of resolve, which is hardwired into our DNA. Stalwart in a belief of all that is right and true and good and kind. Understanding that we are here to fulfill a purpose. Faith is personal and yet connects us to a greater community.

- Hope: A benediction that is fundamental to all human beings. A brightness of spirit. Joyful in the knowledge that optimism and light will prevail. Holding space with optimism for the outcome that will best serve the greater good. Understanding you will be part of the solution. Choosing to see the goodness in people and circumstances that may incite defeatist attitudes in others. Hope motivates us to seek answers and solutions.

- Unfailing: The determination to persevere. To be unafraid of failure. Persistence of spirit. Unwavering in the belief of goodness. A strength of character and the will to honor the truth despite unpopularity. Unwilling to accept defeat in the face of adversity. To resist calls for surrender. Steadfast as you stand in truth.

You may well have your own personal interpretation of each measurement, or you may concur with, or revise, my definitions. I have found Love's Foot Rule to be a most purposeful tool. It is a doctrine to live by and a credo worth honoring with conscious awareness. If it seems overwhelming or insurmountable, don't reflect on the entirety of Love's Foot

Rule. Instead, view each measurement as an aspiration to endeavor: Keep your troubles in perspective and focus with gratitude on what you've got in the moment. You are an adult but, remember, these are tenets by which a child of the 1920s strived to abide. The importance of embracing these beliefs was graciously underscored for me by Ellen.

One Sunday afternoon in January 2017, I was scheduled to facilitate a group event at a beautifully restored 1810s mansion. Upon arrival, I was escorted to a room on the third floor in which I might spend time in reflection prior to the event. The space was warm and welcoming, and before long I sensed a maternal female presence draw near. I was shown a capital letter "E." I sensed that this represented her first initial. Perhaps she had an "E" name, like Eleanor. She was curious about my meditation, so I began to read aloud from the notes I had made about Love's Foot Rule. She then dictated to me her own contribution about a spiritual existence, which I hastily scribbled down. "After a fashion, it is akin to being stricken blind," she said. "It is a matter of adjusting one's orientation to a different way of being, like one who recovers from a debilitation and must learn anew how to speak and move." (When I enquired, the mansion owner told me that the original matriarch was named Ellen.

Unbeknownst to me, the room in which I was meditating was her room.)

What Ellen channeled to me was the essence of a shift that she only achieved with mortal death. She was equating being human with a debilitating experience from which one recovers in Spirit. Her purpose in sharing these thoughts was to inspire us to create the shift *now*. She can seemingly slip between worlds seamlessly. It has become second nature to her. She is attracted to good things as much as she attracts goodness. This is the platform for abundance.

My psychic career is built on the foundation of spiritual trust. Spiritual trust is the foundation from which your good efforts will flow. You can blend the concept of celestial charades with the concept of abundance. These two concepts are not mutually exclusive of one another. They are intertwined if you are willing to avail yourself. You have learned the nuances of receiving information from Spirit. You have read about how Spirit-speak is specific to your personal purview. Now it is time to focus on reciprocating and sending instead of receiving. The difference between taking a risk and making a leap of faith is your degree of spiritual connectivity.

Authenticity begets abundance. Authenticity is a discipline that is achieved by focusing on truth. It begins with self-transparency. Illuminate every corner of your personhood—no secrets of any kind, especially those you keep from yourself—and you will have found the path of true authenticity. Dispense with the victim card. Instead, use your disability or a difficult past as an ability. Be transparent in your truthfulness for having overcome challenges, and your integrity will motivate countless others to do the same. You will have "street credit." Speaking and living the truth is a lifestyle adjustment for some. It is not something you do to get you someplace. It is something you aspire and to embrace because it is the authentic response to your humanity.

You are not charging with undergoing a total overhaul. Nor are you obligated to do anything at all with whatever spiritual gifts you are blessed to receive. Start low and go slow. You may decide to begin by taking an inside-out approach, starting with where you are presently. Who in your immediate environment is in need? Who requires compassion and understanding? Who needs to tell their story to a good listener? This is in keeping with a dream I once had. In it, I was trying to "feel" my way through my basement in pitch-black darkness. I struggled with the disadvantage and a bit of fear. As if to quell my anxiety, I was told, "Be the light." When we become the light, we—literally and figuratively—project a luminosity that brightens our spirit and affects others in ways that are proactive.

Some years back, I had a "chance" encounter with a young man who sat next to me on an airplane. Physically, he was quite handsome, but he also radiated an intangible glow. I was immediately struck with a "knowingness." I felt that he was a good and decent human being who had been successful in life. I also saw his unfulfilled potential to maximize his gifts in service of others. (In my opinion, people who are considered beautiful and successful have an obligation to be especially charitable because our culture tends to magnanimously revere them.) The young man and I struck up a conversation that lead to some meaningful outcomes. Our discussion focused on three principles: educate, enlighten, and empower.

Ignorance need not hold negative connotations. After all, you can only know what you know unless, and until, you know differently. The principle of "educate" or "education" pertains to one's own purpose. It is an understanding of duty to answer the call with reverence. Once you illuminate the truth about yourself, you undergo a transformation. Herein lies an opportunity. That is, when you come to a crossroads, create your own detour and pave a self-directed path.

The principle of enlightenment occurs as a byproduct of the education. When one is engaged in the act of *becoming*, there is a natural desire not only to learn but to *grow*. It is the growing that is the enlightenment. It is a dynamic process of evolution. The enlightenment gives rise to an authentic power of self-actualization. You raise your vibrational frequency such that attunement to playing celestial charades comes effortlessly. And Spirit will lower its vibrational frequency to meet you halfway.

Empowerment refers not only to one's self but the responsibility to empower others with the wisdom and knowledge so accrued. This doesn't mean you risk alienating others by imposing upon them your new plateau of awareness. Be mindful of when, where, and with whom you discuss concepts such as those shared in this book. Be simple and subtle in the context of unique and individual relationships. Channel your energy properly and appropriately. Gauge how much or how little to share based on response and reaction. As much as the act of becoming is a process for you—whether gradual or accelerated—your situation does not directly apply to others' abilities. Allow those so intrigued to find you an accessible mentor in their own time.

My young friend from the airplane never forgot our conversation, and we remain in touch to this day. He is a great athlete and outdoorsman. As his 40th birthday approached, he honored the occasion by hiking up Mt. Rainier. Not only that, he used the hike as an opportunity to solicit financial donors to sponsor the excursion for a charitable cause. He later told me of the many teachable moments that occurred with fellow hikers, previously unknown to him. He has inspired his children. He set an example for his coworkers and community. And he exceeded his financial goal. He is now ever conscious of next steps and new goals for having been educated, enlightened, and empowered.

When you yield and avail yourself to the bounty of all the Universe has to offer, opportunities will begin to find you. My friend recently contacted me with a status report. He has been teaching his oldest daughter to ski, which has reignited his own passion for it. In a casual conversation with a stranger while at their local mountain, the other man suggested that my friend should consider joining the ski patrol. As my friend explained it, the ski patrol has safety as its mission, and is responsible for clearing hazards, searching for lost parties, responding to medical emergencies, and so on.

My friend didn't give it much thought but the very next day, he witnessed an accident at the ski slope and actually provided some assistance. He also found himself searching for two children whose parents reported them missing. As he put it, it seemed as though his next direction was defined and the decision to move forward was made for him. He is now pursuing the opportunity to join the ski patrol officially. It is his goal for the coming year, and will entail additional ski training as well as medical training. This aspiration is a natural extension of what my friend says is "this thing in me for helping people in times of need." Rather than resist or ignore the call, my friend has accepted the invitation to advance by honoring his authenticity.

Attaining authenticity requires that we dispense with inauthenticity. Like my vision of how negative energy is altered and transmuted by Spirit, so can inauthenticity be transformed. Earth will probably always be a place of rivalry and war but that shouldn't be an excuse for hopelessness to pervade. Today, focus on contributing your effort to the good cause. The notion that "nice guys finish last" suggests a race for a prize. But truly kind people wisely accept the graces that come each step of the way. Do your part to dismantle a culture of dysfunction.

Trust your instincts when something seems spiritually amiss, and dismiss with authority any unwanted energies. Disallow negative thoughts from becoming physical ailments, as can happen in those who are petulant and unhappy. Delinquency and criminal activity doesn't always stem from desperation as do boredom and an emptiness for contributing anything of value. For instance, social media is a significant culprit. It encourages narcissism. It facilitates passive-aggressive conduct. It is often a concealment for hateful behavior but it provides a forum for good works too.

Bear in mind that sometimes a setback is really an inspiration in disguise. Assess what doesn't serve you, and seek to dispose of it or transform it into something good. Survey such aspects of your life and think of unconventional means to initiate change. If you are empowered, you will have Spirit as your ally progressing forward. Once you stand in the effervescence of Light and allow its luminosity to infuse you, the sole recourse that exists is but to embrace it and proceed as its bearer.

Abundance and authenticity converge in three new principles: passion, pursuit, and prosperity. Passion is determining what interests, motivates, and inspires you to create and collaborate, like my friend on ski patrol. Those most fortunate among us are employed in the field of personal passion. If you are not so lucky, you can still pursue your passion and become intrigued with following that which calls to you. It's called a hobby. Being passionate can readily parlay into good works, particularly when you are spiritually conscious and aware. We've all heard success stories of people who have parlayed their pivotal circumstances into inspirational ways of earning a living. You may have the idea of launching a new venture or you may channel that passionate energy into something charitable. The choice is entirely your own to make.

Once your passion has been identified, or made itself known to you, the second principle is pursuit. In particular, pursuit is the portion of the process by which you will want to be most closely connected with Spirit. This is seed-and-sow time. Reflect upon the myriad measures Spirit makes to communicate. Be mindful to express thanksgiving every day. Water the idea and encourage its growth by dreaming and visualizing it into fruition. I have manifested entire books and other projects this way. As part of the pursuit, you will wish to be aware of the company you keep. Attracting and connecting to like-minded people is essential. Work your network to build creative momentum that leads to introductions and solid connections. Does your vision require a partner with expertise to complement your own? Or will you fly solo? Listen to constructive critiques but disassociate from those who flagrantly dismiss your dream.

The third principle is prosperity. The average person might equate prosperity with financial success. The wise person equates prosperity with fair and reasonable compensation. I have never had much interest in money. Somehow, someway, I've always had what I've needed. By the same token, I've never wanted to be rich. It always seemed to be an unrealistic aspiration, being rich for the sake of what it gets you. Nor could I conceive the drive some have to win the lottery and become instantly wealthy. I think it would be the worst, most destructive experience in the world. Further, I've never wanted money I haven't personally earned; I would feel so uncomfortable winning the lottery. I only want what's mine because I've worked for it. Behave as if you have just enough to subsist. Frugal and thrifty will serve you well when you feel flush. By the same token, honor your good fortune by giving back. You can do this financially, of course; or this might be an exchange of goods and services by donating your time and volunteering your expertise to others in need.

As you undergo spiritual transformation, you, like I did, stand to lose family or friends who don't like the "new" you. Remain committed and honor your heart. Fear is the only thing preventing you from enacting this process in concert with Spirit. Apathy and procrastination have no place here. I am sometimes disappointed to see clients in follow-up who have not initiated the plan we previously mapped out. It could be as simple as engaging with one's Spirit Guide. And yet here they are, consulting me and wondering why life is still mundane. My job is to work myself out of a job, and nothing makes me prouder than to tell a client, "You no longer need me." Other fear factors are commonplace, such as fear of the unknown or fear of being wrong. Don't forget, this is a partnership. You are not alone on this journey. Spirit is communicating to you if you will only connect the dots to form a complete picture.

Engaging with Spirit in celestial charades is for beginners as much as it is for advanced players. It begins with an open mind and a desire to aspire higher. It is a collaborative process that calls for a braiding of your energy with the divine. You will be poised for success if you know yourself fully and accept all that you are. Believe that you are here for the purpose of contributing something of great value. And know that Spirit awaits you.

Bibliography

ABC News, "PrimeTime: Carrie Fisher Interview." Aired December 21, 2000.

Agnelli, Jarbas, "Birds on the Wires." YouTube, September 6, 2009.

Antinori, Anna, Olivia L. Carter, and Luke D. Smillie. "Seeing it Both Ways: Openness to Experience and Binocular Rivalry Suppression." *Journal of Research in Personality*, 68 (2017): 15–22.

Cabarga, Leslie. *Talks With Trees: A Plant Psychic's Interviews With Vegetables, Flowers and Trees.* Los Angeles: Iconoclassics Publishing Company, 1997.

Cloninger, C. R. *Feeling Good: The Science of Well-Being.* New York: Oxford University Press, 2004.

Emoto, Masaru. *The Hidden Messages in Water.* New York: Atria Books, 2005.

Gagliano, Monica, John C. Ryan, and Patricia Vieira. *The Language of Plants*. Minneapolis, Minn.: University of Minnesota Press, 2017.

Newton, Michael, PhD. *Destiny of Souls: New Case Studies of Life Between Lives*. Woodbury, Minn.: Llewellyn Publications, 2000.

———. *Journey of Souls: Case Studies of Life Between Lives*. Woodbury, Minn.: Llewellyn Publications, 1994.

Robb, Alice. "If Your Name Is Dennis, You're More Likely to Become a Dentist." *New Republic*, January 8, 2014.

Siclari, Francesca, Benjamin Baird, Lampros Perogamvros, Giulio Bernardi, Joshua J LaRocque, Brady Riedner, Melanie Boly, Bradley R Postle, and Giulio Tononi. "The Neural Correlates of Dreaming," *Nature Neuroscience* (online edition), April 10, 2017.

Walker, Jeanne Murray, Ph.D. "Alzheimer's: To Set Them Straight or Not," *Psychology Today* (online edition), October 25, 2013.

Index

About the Author

Psychic medium William Stillman is the internationally known, award-winning author of the *Autism and the God Connection* book trilogy that explores aspects of spiritual giftedness in many people with autism. These books encompass *Autism and the God Connection*, *The Soul of Autism*, and *The Autism Prophecies*. His other books include *Under Spiritual Siege: How Ghosts and Demons Affect Us and How to Combat Them*.

Since 2004, Stillman has worked professionally as a psychic and spiritual counselor. His accuracy in discerning the truth and making predictions that come to fruition has been acclaimed by his clients as truly extraordinary. He has been consulted on missing person and unsolved homicide cases. He also volunteers his time as an investigative resource to the Pennsylvania Paranormal Association.

Stillman has been interviewed on numerous radio shows of a paranormal nature including *Coast to Coast AM*, the most listened to overnight radio program in North America. He has been interviewed on the web series *CharVision* by internationally renowned psychic medium Char Margolis, who called Stillman "really fascinating," and he has been a guest on the popular YouTube series *Swedenborg and Life*. Stillman has been a repeated guest speaker for Lily Dale Assembly near Jamestown, New York, the country's oldest spiritualist community.

Stillman's website is *www.williamstillman.com*.